Advance

T0152465

"Debra Menke's new book, *Powerful Women Plan for Retirement*, is like a good heart-to-heart with your best friend—who happens to be a financial professional. Her straightforward storytelling is a strong cup of coffee waking readers up to the news: the time to start investing in yourself and your retirement is now. Drawing on her own personal story, Debra's book comes from a place of truth and wisdom. The book inspires women to take ownership of their financial futures—and experience the freedom and power that ensue."

– Penny Pennington
Managing partner, Edward Jones

"Money is the number one cause of stress for Americans. Proven strategies to eliminate this stress include education and planning, and this book has both. It's the perfect guide for the modern American woman."

– Dan Miller
Global health and wellness expert

"How many times have you put off your own financial planning because something else seemed more important? As women, we're trained to put others needs ahead of our own. We often help others create their future while ignoring our own. No more. Debbie Menke takes you by the hand to help you plan for your future. With spirit and love, she walks you straight through all the excuses. Excuses like—I'm not good with money, I'll do it later, I need to take care of my kids—these fall by the wayside as she guides you to a powerful vision of your financial future. Read it, do it, and reap the benefits."

– Lisa Earle McLeod
Author of bestselling books, *Selling with Noble Purpose*
and *Leading with Noble Purpose*

"Gritty, authentic and unapologetically real. All growth—be it financial, physical, intellectual, et cetera—begins with the mind, which is not lost on Debbie Menke. This is not just a book that can be applied to the personal finances of women (though it certainly does just that), but her principles should be applied to any person on a development journey. I will buy both my daughters a copy of this book."

– Bill Eckstrom
President, EcSell Institute and author of
bestselling book, *The Coaching Effect*

"This is an unbelievable read for women and men alike. By reading Debbie's book, we are reminded that lessons in fortitude, perseverance and integrity can be learned at any age and at any stage of our lives. Debbie is an excellent businesswoman and more importantly, a genuine human being. Her words will be an inspiration and source of financial wisdom for all who read them. Home run, my friend!"

– Dr. Harry Condoleon
General and cosmetic surgeon

"Being a woman in her fifties, single with twins, and not understanding my journey, this book nailed it. Done with excuses. Time to downsize, stop collecting stuff, make memories, and plan retirement so I can make more memories with my grandchildren. Take Debbie's hand, grab a glass of vino, and enjoy this powerful read."

– Denise LeBeau
Mother and administrative assistant

"Outstanding! This book is a must for women of all ages! I'm married to a financial advisor, yet I've learned so much from Debbie and this book. She has motivated me to get my 'financial house' in better order."

– Carolyn Frakes
Executive assistant

"Debbie's approach to explaining financial planning is a breath of fresh air for women everywhere. From the moment you open this book, you feel the love and care she puts into every page and can't help but feel inspired to take action. This is as much of a spiritual guide to getting to know yourself, as it is an easy to follow step-by-step tool to help you get clear about your finances today, and to plan for the beautiful tomorrow of your dreams. It's a rare and beautiful approach to set the foundation for your financial freedom."

– Annmarie Molina
Founder of SheHaus Coaching

"A complete eye opener! As a self-employed business owner for most of my career, I learned things I wish I would have paid attention to in my twenties. Thanks to Debbie, I now know that it's not too late, and the retirement of my dreams is still very much possible. Debbie's visualizing and meditation exercises are powerful—they really help harness you in and help you get a grasp on where you are and where you ultimately want to be. No matter what age you are, this book is a must read for all women."

– Stephanie Schafer
Business owner

"I've always avoided reading books on finances. However, *Powerful Women Plan for Retirement* is a book I will read again and again and will share with all the special women in my life. Debbie does such a great job simplifying the concept of 'financial planning.' She turns the terrifying thoughts of saving, paying off debt, and preparing for retirement, into actionable steps and even makes the process fun. Thank you, Debbie, for giving us F.R.E.E.D.O.M!"

– Cristy Monteiro
Senior business development, SkinCeuticals

"Bursting with hope, no matter where you are at in your journey. The sparkling fresh perspective and pure positive life-giving exercises in this book will help you build a foundation of peace and financial power. Simply a must read!"

– Tamberly Auer
Account executive

"*Powerful Women Plan for Retirement* is written in a way that is so down to earth and easy to read that it will draw you in and excite you with ideas for your financial future. This book isn't just for the woman who has retirement in her near future; it's for anyone looking for guidance, advice and financial education. *Powerful Women Plan for Retirement* is a book I will pass on to all women in my life. Everyone deserves to be a Powerful Woman!"

– Paige Baade
Paige Baade Photography

"What a breath of fresh air. I loved this book! Debbie is a gifted writer. Her approach is refreshing. Retirement is not an easy subject to cover or explain. She shares her knowledge in a way that is easy for anyone to understand and infuses it with love and light. Thanks for speaking my language, Debbie."

– Kim Weaver
Author, and intuitive expert and coach

"Debbie Menke is a trailblazer in financial planning and education for women. I wish I had this guidance twenty years ago, but grateful to know that it's not too late. I am motivated in a way that I didn't even know was possible and cannot wait to share this amazing read with my 'powerful women' tribe. Thank you for empowering me to change my story."

– Tania Moffett- Hilber
Account executive

"Intuitive. Bold. Daring. Brave. Debbie shares lessons that will benefit powerful women everywhere."

— **Darla McEnroe**
LMSW

"Debbie's gift of knowledge, wisdom, and love radiates her truest desire for others to gain (in one package) what is much needed in our societal awareness of mind, body, spirit connection. Not only does she address financial success, she embraces the entire woman and her need for comfort, peace, and balance. Debbie explains financial mysteries in a way that can be understood clearly and easily. She embraces many avenues of inner and outer growth which connect us to a divine union of the soul— leaving us with peace of mind, financial health and wellbeing. Ah, sleep at last!"

— **Margi Lantos**
Intuitive consultant, Spiritual Bridges

Powerful Women Plan for Retirement

POWERFUL WOMEN

PLAN FOR RETIREMENT

TAKE **OWNERSHIP** OF YOUR **FINANCIAL FUTURE**

DEBRA K. MENKE

NEW YORK

LONDON • NASHVILLE • MELBOURNE • VANCOUVER

Powerful Women Plan for Retirement

Take Ownership of Your Financial Future

Published in New York, New York, by Morgan James Publishing. Morgan James is a trademark of Morgan James, LLC. www.MorganJamesPublishing.com

ISBN 9781631950292 paperback
ISBN 9781631950308 eBook
Library of Congress Control Number: 2020932833

Cover Design Concept: Jennifer Stimson

Cover and Interior Design: Chris Treccani www.3dogcreative.net

Editor: Cory Hott

Author Photo: Paige Baade

Book Coaching: The Author Incubator

Morgan James is a proud partner of Habitat for Humanity Peninsula and Greater Williamsburg. Partners in building since 2006.

Get involved today! Visit
MorganJamesPublishing.com/giving-back

For Mom and Dad.

Thank you for giving me the sacred gift of family and for always believing in me and my crazy dreams. You are the reason I am who I am today. Without you choosing me and loving me unconditionally, I am not sure where I would have ended up. I dedicate this book to you both—my inspiration, my rocks, and my glue.

Table of Contents

Foreword

When people ask me who inspires me, my answer is always the same, "The women who work with me. And there are 150 of them." Many of them are the family breadwinners or single mothers or both. Before they come to work, I know they've dressed the kids, provided breakfast, met the school bus, fed the dog, done chores, run errands, checked in with aging parents, and got themselves ready to show up for work on time prepared to give their all. I don't know how they do it, but they do. And there always seems to be something left over to nurture colleagues who might need it.

I know what they haven't done. They haven't spent fifteen minutes on their own wellbeing or spent a moment thinking about their financial future.

Debbie Menke was one of those women. I thought I knew her reasonably well over ten years of sharing cosmetic adventures with her, but after reading her book, I realize that I'd only scratched the surface. You will learn as I did, that here is a story that screams "If Debbie can do it, then so can I."

Do what? Survive being given up for adoption as a baby; marriage to an alcoholic drug addict; a second marriage that also ended in divorce; building a successful business and then watching it dissolve as a town took sides in her divorce;

postpartum depression; the responsibility of raising five children alone, one of whom was born with half a heart; desperately looking for a job so she could pay for her sick child's medical expenses and the other essentials of life, like putting food on the table.

It's a dramatic story that has a happy ending because Debbie finally takes responsibility for her life and realizes that nobody is doing it to her. She is the master of her own creation. Where she finds herself is the result of the choices she and only she made. Once she comes to that conclusion, she finds ways to turn negatives into positives, failures into successes (astonishing successes), and a future of insecurity into one of emotional and financial stability. Using her personal story, a significant part of which I was privileged to share with her, she guides us through the practices and tools she uses to change her life.

For example, have you ever done a budget? Household expenses, personal expenses, professional expenses. Do you know how to put one together and the purpose it serves? I know, I hate the word budget, too. The meetings I dread the most are the ones where we sit around a table pulling a budget apart. But it's the only way to have any control over your life and the future. Do you know how to save for an emergency fund? Do you even know what constitutes a financial emergency? And if you have put some money together, do you know what to do with it? Do you know how to stop the world for 15 minutes and nurture body and soul so that you're so much more effective to yourself and those around you? Debbie answers all those questions and more as she walks us carefully through a blueprint for financial security. She has seen too many women wanting to retire, play with their grandchildren, travel, experience more of life, who are reduced to living on their social security and a depleted 401K.

I wish I had read this book 25 years ago when I started my company. Perhaps I could have spared myself the sleepless nights consumed by the "Are we going to make it?" nightmare. I did read a book about visualizations (one of Debbie's important tools). I learned that if you can feel it, touch it, smell it and experience it in your mind, you can bring it into reality. When I first started my company, I used to wait anxiously for the mail and then drive to the bank with any checks that arrived. (I needed to do this promptly because there was a good chance that the check I'd written for food the day before was going to bounce!) When I learned about visualization, instead of tossing and turning with anxiety in bed, I closed my eyes and imagined myself driving to the bank—getting into my car, turning it on, the crunch of gravel under the tires as I drove out, the hum of the engine, the sound of the indicators, the feel of pulling up at the bank's drive-in window, handing over checks and a deposit slip, and then looking at the receipt. I visualized seeing $30,000. $30,000! A far cry from what was really in there. The feeling I had was so intense that from that moment on, I knew success was possible and I could bring it into reality. And, with the help of people like Debbie, we did, including distribution in fifty countries.

Along the way, it's been obvious to me that even the smartest of women, don't plan for the future. I didn't. I just assumed that somehow things would work out. That wasn't very smart. This book will show you how small and simple changes can make a huge difference not only to your future but the future of your family. And it will require you to be selfish. Yes, that's hard for women, but get your own house in order first and then you can help others. For many women, it's the other way around. And it doesn't work. Debbie has daily experience of this in her counseling of women who are struggling to provide for their futures.

This firsthand knowledge is what led Debbie to write a book for women. A book that is full of concrete information regarding investing (always a mystery to me); tools that help you to grow in confidence, not only in a material sense but also a spiritual one, and a book that is full of love, respect and encouragement for women of all economic situations. It's true that the financial world has been the domain of men for far too long. Debbie and her colleagues are changing that. So can you.

– Jane Iredale
Founder of Iredale Cosmetics, Inc.

Introduction

It is 2019 and the financial industry is still a male-dominated industry. Yet change is coming driven by women who no longer want to be kept in the dark about their own or their families' finances. Women who are taking charge of their future and have plans, big plans, for a safe and exciting retirement. They're taking ownership and being aided in their quest by women who've had the courage to break through into the world of finance and make it their own.

My goal in writing this book is to help and encourage *you* to take ownership. It isn't difficult. It can be fun, rewarding, and satisfying, not to mention it can make it easier to sleep at night.

I've had the opportunity to travel extensively over the past fifteen years. I've had the honor and privilege to meet, lead, and collaborate with countless successful women. They are some of the most talented and powerful women in the country, yet for all of that, few have taken ownership of their financial futures. This not only impacts them, but generations to come. My vision is that, with the right support, education, and coaching, we have an opportunity to make real and lasting change, one powerful woman at a time. I want you to be one of those women.

This book is my love letter to you. To all of you powerful women (whether you know it or not) who are ready to be the master of your own fate and take charge of your financial future. You have this book in your hands, which tells me that you're ready. You're ready to tap into your ability to visualize and manifest the future you want. And because we're women, we know that life isn't only about the physical; it has to be supported by spiritual strength. This is what produces lasting results that can withstand the ups and downs of a full life.

This book gives you practical financial advice and supports it with techniques for developing that spiritual strength. It is my hope that you will allow me to lead the way so that you can do the same for the ones you love. I want to make a difference in your life and the lives of your family for generations to come. Let's create a movement.

Welcome to the Powerful Women Tribe!

Health, wealth, and happiness,

Debra K. Menke

Chapter 1:

The Dilemma

"Risk comes from not knowing what you're doing."
~ **Warren Buffett**

Madeline's Story

Madeline turned fifty this year. She is an intelligent and successful businesswoman. She travels the globe and has had amazing experiences during her career. She is single and has been divorced twice. She has not been successful in the love department, but she kills it at work. She loves to entertain and knows how to throw a fabulous party. She is one of the best friends a girl could ask for and, honey, she loves her eighties music.

Did I mention she had just turned fifty?

Throughout her career, Madeline made many strategic career moves, each job paying her more than the last. She's highly sought after in her field.

She probably had about four different 401K plans out there, ballpark of about $400K total. During her earlier years, she didn't contribute as much as she should have. But she got closer to retirement and saw the value of maxing out her retirement plan as best she could.

Madeline was sick of the grind. She was in and out of airports, traveling to a different city every week. She was on her laptop and cell phone 24/7. She was not as young as she once was, and she felt it. Good thing she tried to keep herself up by getting to the gym every morning because she had terrible eating habits due to her travel schedule and drank a diet coke (a forty-four ouncer) for breakfast just to get herself going. And please don't preach to her because she was not giving it up.

She had no idea how much money she was spending, but she knew it was way too much. Madeline owned a gorgeous home in the Berkshires, but her mortgage was high and she was paying so much money just to live in her home that she had little money left over for anything else at the end of the month. I call this phenomenon, "house poor." She owned some other real estate which should be paid off this year. She worshiped the sun, loved to golf, and did I mention that she can throw a heck of a party?

Faced with the reality that retirement somehow crept up on her (and believe me, she did not want to keep working past age sixty—unless it was on her terms), she felt extremely stressed out and ill-prepared. She had no idea if she would have enough money to quit her job. She knew she needed help and knew she needed to get her act together and create a plan so that she could get off the hamster wheel and enjoy her life.

Is there any part of this story that sounds familiar to you? How is it possible that as women, we can rule the world, kick butt, take names, raise our families, run companies? You are putting out fires and saving the day for everyone else, yet in many cases, you haven't put your oxygen mask on first—most of you don't have a solid plan in place and have no idea how to retire. Will you have enough income coming in to be able to quit your job? Where will the income come from? How does this stuff work? Nobody taught it to you in school. Nobody sat down with you when you took your first job and told you how it all works.

I have had this same conversation with countless women—again: successful, gorgeous, talented women. Women who look like they have got their act together. These are the women you are jealous of. On the outside, their lives look perfect. Yet, they are dying on the inside and they have no idea what to do about their finances.

You are making most of the buying decisions, you are running other people's companies and making them money, but you have no idea how to take care of yourself. You weren't taught to take care of yourself. You were taught to be obedient and to take care of everyone else's needs first.

You are making great money, yet you are not taking care of your money. You are leaving the decisions to your husbands and fathers and boyfriends. It's time to rise and take ownership of your financial future.

We started our careers worried about making the highest possible salary, got married, some of us had children (I had five) some of us got divorced (I did twice). And we've been living our lives, taking care of everyone else but ourselves. Much of the time, we have just put it on auto-pilot and plowed through the day. Days turned into months; months turned into years. We measured the months and years by deadlines and sales goals. By career and family milestones.

Now here you are. You are fifty(-ish) (I love being fifty-ish, by the way). I am the best version of myself that I've ever been. But with that, don't you find that you just don't want to work as hard as you have been? Have you noticed that your desires are shifting? I'm starting to care less about things and more about quality experiences with the people I love. Have you started thinking it may be time to downsize your life as opposed to collecting more stuff? Are you finding yourself dreaming of a debt-free life? Is that new designer handbag really that important to you?

Even five years ago, I was in a completely different space in my life. Do we somehow magically transform into a true adult at fifty(-ish)? I'm not sure. But I am sure of one thing—it's time for you to make a plan so that you're not sitting here at sixty(-ish) wondering if you're going to be financially secure enough to quit your job or if you'll have to continue working for another ten years because you didn't take the time to put a solid plan in place.

At this point you may start to panic. You may even beat yourself up (we're good at that). But please don't do that. In fact, I'd like you to do the opposite. Right here. Right now. I want you to stop. Put your hand on your heart and take three deep breaths. Repeat after me: I am right where I need to be. Everything is always working out for me.

Please speak kindly to yourself. You are right where you need to be. Somehow, you were led to pick up this book. You belong to the tribe of other fifty (-ish) women looking for answers. You've obviously realized you need a little help. Good for you. You've got this. Take my hand—you're probably doing better than you think you are. Just breathe. We can do this thing together. And at the end of it, we'll pour a glass of champagne and make a toast to your new plan—a plan that will lead you on the path to living the retirement of your daydreams.

Let's take away all of the stress of not having a financial plan in place and work on creating a bulletproof plan. Let's get you moving into the next ten years with style, grace, and attitude, fully knowing that ten years from now, when you find yourself at sixty(-ish), you can smile, pop another bottle of champagne (perhaps even a bottle of Dom) and say, "see ya" to that career.

I've been right where you are, and for that reason, I'm excited to be a part of your journey.

Chapter 2:

The Story

"Our deepest fear is not that we are inadequate. Our deepest fear is that we are powerful beyond measure. It is our light, not our darkness that most frightens us. We ask ourselves, Who am I to be brilliant, gorgeous, talented, fabulous? Actually, who are you not *to be? You are a child of God. Your playing small does not serve the world. There is nothing enlightened about shrinking so that other people won't feel insecure around you. We are all meant to shine, as children do. We were born to make manifest the glory of God that is within us. It's not just in some of us; it's in everyone. And as we let our own light shine, we unconsciously give other people permission to do the same. As we are liberated from our own fear, our presence automatically liberates others."*

~ Marianne Williamson

It may seem to an outside observer that I was born with a silver spoon. However, my beginning was a little rough. I was born in Atlanta, Georgia. My biological mother grew up in Louisiana and was sent away to a home for unwed mothers after being the victim of date rape in college. She was sent away by her parents, who did not want anyone in the town to know that she was pregnant. That's what they did in 1969. Shortly after my birth, I was put up for adoption. I realize now that the Universe was lining everything up so that Denis Menke, an MLB player for the Atlanta Braves, and his wife, Jean would walk into the adoption agency after baseball season ended, ready to adopt me. Dad tells the story that I had a terrible cold (snotty nose) and was wearing a little pink dress that was three sizes too big for me. He said he knew that I was his little girl the first time he laid eyes on me.

I grew up in Major League Baseball parks. Dad played baseball for the Milwaukee Brewers, Atlanta Braves, Houston Astros, and even played in the '72 World Series as a part of the Big Red Machine with the Cincinnati Reds—alongside Pete Rose and Johnny Bench.

My parents adopted me because they were unable to have children of their own. After they brought me home, my brother Scott came along followed by my little sister, Kristina. Dad always told me, "Debbie, God wanted us to have you first." I'm forty-nine years old and I never tire of hearing him tell me that story.

Life was good. I had a fun and easy childhood. Dad was gone for about eight months out of the year during baseball season and every summer as soon as school ended, my mom would pack up the station wagon and we would head to Houston to be with dad. I know that I am a strong woman because I grew up with a strong woman. Mom was the unsung hero in our family and the glue that held all of us together and still does to this day.

During the summers, we lived in an apartment close to the Astrodome. We spent our days playing at the pool while mom worshiped the sun and dad routinely went to the ballpark by at least noon for batting practice with the team. In the afternoon, we would all get a shower, get dressed up and head to the ballpark for the game. Yes, dressed up, to the nines. We sat in the section of the ballpark reserved for Astros' family members. Mom always played the part of a player's wife. She was always dressed beautifully—gorgeous long legs and fabulous heels; we wore heels to the ballpark.

Although my brother and sister ran around the stadium each night, as the oldest, whether I was expected to or not, I played my part and pretended to be more mature and sat with Mom. I remember from an early age wanting to be perfect, wanting to look perfect and act perfect in order to make my mom and dad proud of me. Many evenings, I would sit with Carmen Berra—Yogi Berra's wife. She was so kind to me, and she was one of those women who just seemed to draw you in and make you feel special. She was a gracious, beautiful, and caring woman. She and Yogi gave me a card for my high school graduation with my first $100 bill. I will never forget the feeling of opening that card and how awesome it felt to have my own $100 bill.

"Love is the most important thing in the world,
but baseball is pretty good, too."
— Yogi Berra

Celebration

If you've ever attended a Houston Astros winning game, you'd know that as is tradition, "Celebration" by Kool and the Gang blasts throughout the stadium. When we lost, it was pretty quiet in the stands.

Either way, at the end of the game, we would make our way through all of the fans, into the private elevator that led us through the tunnels and into the family waiting room where all the other wives and kids waited for their superstar dads and husbands.

Dad was almost always the last one out of the clubhouse, especially when we lost. But, when he would emerge (after what seemed like hours), we would walk with him out to the car and as soon as we exited the stadium, he would be swarmed by fans asking for his autograph. Strangers asked for my daddy's autograph. I can't tell you how it felt to stand by Dad's side while droves of men, women, and children handed him their precious cards and balls and waited in line for his signature. I think I stood taller, and leaned in closer to him as if they were asking for my autograph. As if to say, "That's my Dad." As if I had done something to deserve the attention. As if I were special just because I belonged to him. The experience was intoxicating, and it was one of my favorite baseball rituals. I remember how people looked at me as if sizing me up. I think they were wondering what it was like to be the child of an MLB athlete. Perhaps they could tell how proud I was to stand next to him, and how wonderful it felt to be his daughter.

Those memories, although fun to reminisce about, played an integral part in shaping who I am today. I think they made me crave perfection and crave big experiences.

Sweet Sixteen

When I turned sixteen, my dad bought me a brand new, cherry red convertible. I was one of the oldest in my grade and that car made me feel cool and gave the impression (in my mind) that we were wealthy. I never had a shortage of friends who wanted to cruise Clearwater Beach on the weekends and flirt with boys on the strip. Boys would jump into my car to meet us. Dad loved cars, and the new car smell brings me back to those happy memories of my teenage years. Isn't it amazing how a smell can bring back a memory? And how you can associate the feelings you felt even thirty years ago to things in your present? Remember that—it will be important in a later chapter.

Work Ethic

Although it may appear that I was given everything I wanted, I developed a good work ethic at a young age. I started babysitting kids in the neighborhood when I was about eleven years old. Dad taught me how to mow our lawn with the push mower, and I mowed lawns in the neighborhood for money. I also became a lifeguard at the pool (which was a great fit, because I am a mermaid). I even worked as a salad bar girl at Wendy's and, shortly after, landed the most coveted job of all, the sales job at The Limited in Countryside Mall. That was my first experience with sales. And I was good at it. I kept a notebook of all my customers with their sizes, and favorite colors and styles. I called them on a regular basis and built a following. Plus, I had full access to a gorgeous new wardrobe as a sixteen-year-old. My love for fashion and beauty had its beginnings.

After graduating from high school, I was accepted into Florida State University. I pledged Alpha Gamma Delta and proceeded to party in true Seminole fashion over the next year. I had no idea what I wanted to do with my life. I had my first taste of freedom and I just wanted to play. That year, I met my first husband—in a bar. I fell in love the instant I looked into his eyes, and also fell quickly into a toxic relationship that revolved around partying and drinking, and since that was what everyone else around us was doing, I didn't realize that he had a serious problem with alcohol and, I would later find out, drug abuse.

Babies and Financial Trouble

By age twenty-one, I had my first child. Ryan Christopher was born, and he was beautiful and perfect. Thirteen months later, at twenty-two, Cori Lynn (my gorgeous little redhead) was born. After Cori's birth, I experienced severe postpartum depression and ended up in a psychiatric unit for three days because I couldn't stop crying. Back in the nineties, I had not heard of postpartum depression, and I'm not sure anyone around me even knew what it was. I felt like there was something seriously wrong with me. It was a terrible and horrifying experience to be locked up at twenty-two years old, surrounded by severely mentally ill human beings, especially after giving birth just days before. After recovering from that experience, I found myself pregnant again nineteen months later, and my third child, Kyle Wilson was born. The date was December 2, 1994—that day my life changed forever.

Kyle was born with hypoplastic left heart syndrome, a severe congenital heart abnormality. I was twenty-three years old. I had three babies under the age of three. My husband was an alcoholic and drug addict. How did this happen to me?

Three Choices

Within hours of Kyle's birth, he was transported to Cincinnati Children's Hospital (just over the river), where they gave me the devastating news of his condition and odds of his survival.

Dr. Alan Mendelsohn, a kind cardiologist, sat me down and gave me three options.

1. I could allow Kyle to die peacefully.
2. I could put him on the list for a heart transplant.
3. I could choose a series of three open-heart surgeries, which were fairly new at the time and would require us to be flown, via medical Learjet, to the University of Michigan in Ann Arbor.

My Life Would Never Be the Same

Shortly after Kyle was taken to Cincinnati Children's Hospital, I found myself home alone with the babies, no idea where my husband was (which was fairly typical). I put Ryan (three) and Cori Lynn (two) to bed. I waited for my mom to fly in to help me because Kyle was lying in a hospital bed waiting for me to make a decision on what course of action to take. I got the babies to sleep and dragged myself into my bed, still sore from my thirty-hour labor and delivery, and I proceeded to cry like I've never cried before in my life. I remember trying to muffle the sounds of my crying into my pillow so that I didn't wake up the babies. The muffled sounds were more like groans than a cry.

How did this happen? My perfect baby? They had to cut open my baby's chest? His heart? How is this possible? Why me? How am I equipped to make that decision? I am twenty-three years old. I have three children. All babies. I am alone. Let my baby die? No. Have a heart transplant? Yes. I'm not going to make him go through three surgeries. No way am I going to put him through that.

The crying went on for hours and hours and hours until a strange sense of peace and calm came over me and entered my bedroom. A peace that I cannot describe. It was as if I was enveloped in complete warmth and love. I tried to lift my head from the pillow to see, but the light in the room was blinding; I was no longer in my bedroom. I had somehow been transported into what I can only describe as a heavenly place filled with pure positive energy and love. At that moment, I knew that somehow Kyle was going to be okay. And I fell asleep for the first time in what seemed like days.

When I woke up the next morning, I knew that I was supposed to choose the new series of three open-heart surgeries. When I told Dr. Mendelsohn my decision later that day, he told me that Kyle probably would have died waiting on an infant heart (I didn't know it at the time, but there are few infant hearts available and many beautiful souls who are waiting on the list).

My mom flew to the rescue to pick up Ryan and Cori Lynn, and took them back to Florida while I flew in the medical Learjet with Kyle to the University of Michigan. He had his first open-heart surgery at eight days old. I spent a couple of months living at the Ronald McDonald House in Ann Arbor. Alone. It was Christmas. It was 1994. I had no money and was grateful for the many people who donated meals to the Ronald McDonald house over those terrifying months.

Kyle had his next open-heart surgery at six months old and his third surgery at eighteen months old.

I later found out that in addition to Kyle's congenital heart abnormality, he was also diagnosed with Klippel Feil Syndrome, a severe form of scoliosis that, in later years, resulted in multiple spinal surgeries. Today, Kyle has a spinal fusion with titanium rod from his hips to his neck.

I grew up quickly that year. Kyle was so weak that he was unable to take a bottle; I had to feed him through an NG tube at home. When we weren't living in a hospital, he was being monitored 24/7 with in-home nursing care. During this time, I was forced to sign up for Medicaid and food stamps in order to care for my children.

Divorce and Bankruptcy

I ended up moving back to Florida to be closer to my parents so that I didn't have to do it all alone, and I finally made the decision to divorce in 1995. I was unable to care for three babies and an alcoholic at the same time. My partying days were over, and I had turned into a full-time nurse and mother.

After thirteen months of Kyle being too weak to drink a bottle, he had to go through another expensive surgery at which time they placed a feeding tube directly through his abdomen and into his stomach. One night I had a dream that Kyle's tube had fallen out of his stomach and was lying in his crib. The scar was completely healed and he was able to eat. When I woke up in the morning, I went into his room, and as God as my witness, his feeding tube had somehow come out of his tummy (which is practically impossible because there was a balloon on the inside to keep that from happening). Yet, the tube was lying in his crib. And even more incredibly, the area of his tummy that just hours before had a tube through it was completely healed over. It looked like there had been a scar there for years. No blood. No scabs. No wound. Healed. I called my mother who rushed over. We made him a little peanut butter sandwich and he has been eating us out of house and home ever since.

Throughout most of that, we didn't have any health insurance, and somehow, even after the Medicaid benefits kicked in, I still owed $600K for Kyle's millions of dollars in surgical care. There I was. Alone. With three babies. One who could die at any minute. And I had now filed for bankruptcy.

By 1998, I was learning to live my new normal.

Farm Life and Success

Three years after my divorce, I packed up my children for the summer and we went to visit my Grandma Mary, who lived in the small farming community of Bancroft, Iowa. Dad grew up there and was drafted right out of high school by the Milwaukee Braves and signed a contract right there on his parents' farm. It didn't take long for me to catch the attention of a hardworking, local farm boy and before long we were married, and I was pregnant with my fourth child, my little farmer, Nicholas. I can see clearly now that I was exhausted from caring for three babies on my own and was desperate for someone to help me raise my children. Kyle's surgeries and the resulting financial struggle had taken its toll. And as a young woman, I had also bought into the idea that women needed to be married with a family in order to live a fulfilling life.

I must confess I did not make a good farmer's wife. Picture Zsa Zsa Gabor on *Green Acres*.

Living in a town of 800 people in the middle of rural Iowa after traveling the country in style, being used to fine dining and having incredibly big experiences, I was bored out of my mind. As a result, I began to create my idea of a dream business, a day spa (because why wouldn't I open an amazing spa in a town of 800 people in the middle of a cornfield and a bean field). Perhaps because there was nowhere to get a good facial, massage, mani, or pedi. And I just knew that if I was starving for the experience of luxury and self-care, all the other women in the area must be too. I purchased an old paint store on Main Street, gutted the building, hired a contractor, and went to work creating Spa Dee Dah.

I hired the most incredible staff, and even recruited an aesthetician from Minneapolis and convinced her to move to Iowa and join my team. It was gorgeous, and the energy was amazing. I purchased a targeted mailing list and sent out free massages, manis, pedis, facials to hundreds of women in a sixty-mile radius. I knew that if they came in to visit us just once, they would fall in love with their *experience* and would become a regular client. I was right.

Because of my love for retail, I brought in products that you couldn't find anywhere else in our area (at that time). Beautiful, high-end, results-oriented products.

We carried *jane iredale* mineral cosmetics, Prive hair care, and Dermalogica. Now remember, the year was 2001, and these products were the best of the best. To this day, I guarantee you won't find a better cosmetic line that *jane iredale*.

People thought I was crazy.

I kept saying, "If you build it, they will come." (When in Iowa, think Field of Dreams, right? Giggle.)

Well, they came. From everywhere. Minneapolis, Des Moines, even Chicago—all over! Spa Dee Dah was a huge success until postpartum depression struck again.

My fifth child, Riley Denis, was born in August of that year. Postpartum depression hit me even harder this time. I could barely function. I couldn't get out of bed. I felt like I was in a deep, dark, slimy pit of despair and had no idea how to get out of it. My weight was at an all-time high. I had five children. An amazing business. And a farm family who did not seem to understand me. The depression got so bad that I went from one anti-depressant to another and my world spiraled out of control.

God Intervened in the Garage

One afternoon after work, I pulled into the garage and closed the door behind me. The car was still running. I just sat there. Paralyzed. No emotion. Completely numb. I have no idea how long I sat there but I would have stayed; I think I would have stayed there. I just couldn't see a way out.

I heard a voice say to me "Get out of the car, and go inside to your children. You do not want them to find you out here. Get out of the car now."

I shut the car off, walked inside, and I'm not sure I ever told anyone about what I had *almost* done. That day, I just wanted to die. I just wanted a way out of my pain.

I wish I could say that things turned around that day and that God magically transported me from my depression and we all lived happily ever after. But it got so much worse.

Since this is my story, I am not going to place any blame on anyone else. I am going to take responsibility for my story.

Many evenings, I stayed at the spa to avoid going home to deal with my marriage and the utter exhaustion that I felt from taking care of five small humans. Let me tell you, there are no words to describe how much I love those five humans, but I was so depressed that I couldn't handle even the smallest tasks like dishes and diapers.

At the spa, I was surrounded by beauty and customers who were in love with their experience. It was the only place I felt like I belonged, felt good, felt valued. Felt like I was going to make it? Live through it? I don't know. I know that it wasn't easy to live with me. I know that I wasn't being the mother I needed to be. I was depressed, exhausted, and I was trying to escape a marriage that I never should have gotten myself into. Honestly, the thought of moving to the small town my father grew up in seemed like a romantic thing to do. It seemed like a safe and perfect place to raise my children. And when this man showed up, offering me a stable home, community, and the financial stability that I needed after having to declare bankruptcy and after years of taking care of my children alone, I accepted the help. The problem was neither of us married for the right reasons.

Losing My Business

In 2005, I went through my second divorce. In a small town, people take sides. My husband was part of the community long before I was. I'd come in with three children, had two more, and then divorced. As a result of our divorce, my spa business tanked, and it happened fast. All fifteen staff walked out on me the same day. Someone got a hold of my client list and canceled 367 clients in a matter of three days. I had a gorgeous spa for sale in the middle of nowhere and ended up selling it at a $60,000 loss. Even my best friends turned their backs on me and took my husband's side. In their defense, they saw that I was a complete mess and not handling the depression well. Again, this is me owning my own stuff.

There I was with five young children. Approximately $500 to my name. No job. And it felt like I was the most hated and talked about woman in town. I didn't even want to go to the grocery store. I felt like I lived in a fishbowl. The pain was indescribable. How did my life come to this? And more importantly, how was I going to make it through this? When would this pain end?

God Sent Me an Angel

In 2006, I heard that Jane Iredale was going to be making a rare personal appearance at a brunch being held for spa owners in the Minneapolis area. I knew I needed to be there. I knew I was supposed to work for her company.

I attended the brunch and was able to introduce myself to Jane. I told her that I had carried her products in my spa, Spa dee dah. Jane told me that she knew of my spa and as it turns out, I had no idea that we had been one of the top retailers in the Midwest at that time. I told her about my situation and let her know that it was my desire to work for her. A few months later, I became the *jane iredale* Sales Consultant for Iowa, Illinois, and Nebraska. I traveled all over those three states. By then, Dad had retired from baseball. Mom and Dad took turns flying up to help me with the kids. I traveled three weeks at a time and then worked from my home office for three weeks before mom or dad came back up to help so I could get back on the road again. We did this for years when the kids were young. I cannot imagine what I would have done without the support of my parents.

Two years later, I was promoted to regional director for the Midwest. And a year after that, to regional director for the Central US. It wasn't long before I was asked to take the coveted position of director of sales, U.S. and Caribbean. I was good at what I did and felt good in my skin again.

When I began working for Jane, I was finally making money. I had a 401K plan. I had an amazing insurance policy through work (which was incredibly important because of

Kyle's continued surgeries, hospital, and doctor bills) and I was able to provide health insurance for all five of my children.

At that point, I was on the road flying across the country every other week. I was racking up Delta miles and Hilton points. I led a team of approximately seventy, which included six regional directors, forty-two sales consultants, and other educational support staff across the country. I was well-respected, and I loved being of service to the women on my team (and a few men, too). I considered myself a servant leader. I truly wanted to make a difference to Jane's organization and to the women I served in that role.

During my tenure at *jane iredale*, I made an extraordinary income. I purchased a beautiful six-bedroom home and was able to provide a comfortable life for my children. I will confess however, that I spent way too much money. I had a personal shopper at Nordstrom, I bought only designer clothes, Louis Vuitton handbags, and spent money on Botox and other cosmetic procedures in order to look the part. The women I was hiring kept getting younger and younger, and I was now in my mid-forties. The only financial decision I made right during that time was to max out my 401k plan every year.

I was the director of sales in charge of our entire domestic sales team. I was tasked with setting our sales targets and goals, annual expense budgets—in charge of millions of dollars in annual sales revenue, made most of our hiring and firing decisions, led national sales meetings, reported our weekly progress in the boardroom with the rest of the executive management team every Tuesday morning—and acted as head cheerleader for everyone along the way! Yet, I was not taking ownership of my financial future and had no idea how to plan for retirement. I was taking care of an entire organization of women. Leading the charge. But I had not put my oxygen mask on. Remember—I told you I've been in your shoes. I've got your number, and even better, I've got your back.

The Universe Designs a Major Shift in Careers

One afternoon after a meeting, my executive assistant invited me to a Superbowl party they were having. Her husband was a financial advisor and, long story short, he introduced me to the opportunity of going to work with his brokerage firm. After studying thirteen-hour days for my securities exams and learning the industry, I began my new career as a financial professional. As I'm sure you can imagine, it didn't take long for me to realize that I had been spending way too much money and saving too little. I quickly made the decision to take control of my financial future and created what I lovingly refer to as my F.R.E.E.D.O.M. plan.

I believe that every step along my journey, although difficult, has led me to exactly where I am supposed to be today in this moment, writing this book as a love letter to you. I have a greater purpose, and I want to make a difference. Through all of my experiences, I have earned the right to be here and have a sincere passion and desire to help you. I have an understanding of how to reach you right where you are, without judgment. And I have the ability to sit down and explain things to you in a way that is simple for you to understand. I sincerely want to help you to achieve your financial goals and to have a basic understanding of the things we should all know and weren't taught.

Today, I spend most of my time helping people with retirement planning as well as coaching them on how to accumulate and build wealth. I teach people how to prepare for retirement as well as how to create a strategic stream of income during retirement so they can live the life of their dreams.

Over the years, I have met countless professional women who have no understanding of how to prepare themselves for the future. Women who are ten to fifteen years away from retirement and not sure what to do in order to get there. Women who are afraid to ask questions of male advisors, husbands, or fathers. Women who appear to have it all together on the outside but feel completely inadequate when it comes to their finances. Beautiful, successful, intelligent, creative, amazing women.

It is for these women (my tribe) that I have captured my story on paper. It is my mission to help you understand how to take ownership of your financial future.

If any of this resonates with you please, come as you are, go make yourself a cup of coffee, and let's sit down together and make a plan. If I can do it, I promise you can too. And you'll probably do it in a much more elegant and effortless way than I did.

I love coaching and mentoring women in the area of finance and feel like I am making a difference that will have a ripple effect for generations to come. It is my sincere desire that you find something in my story that inspires you to show up for yourself in a new way. I continue to write my story—and each chapter gets better and better. And yours can too!

Chapter 3:

The Journey to Freedom

"Financial freedom is freedom from fear."
~ **Robert Kiyosaki**

By now, you're beginning to take inventory on where you are on your journey. We all have our own stories. And you are either thinking to yourself, "Dang, I've led a pretty good life—that girl was a complete mess." Or, you're resonating with some part of my story and thinking we could grab a cup of coffee together and compare notes. Either way, I hope you trust that not only do God and the Universe have your back, but that I also have your back. I want you to succeed. I want to help you to live your life on your terms—a life full of freedom.

Have you ever gotten in your car and drove across the country? I've taken some pretty long road trips in the past. My last "road trip," though, was a four-hour trip from Las Vegas to the Grand Canyon. My sweetheart and I were in Vegas for a long weekend and I decided that it would be cool to hike the

Grand Canyon, so we rented a car, entered the address into the GPS, and started driving.

As you know, road trips can be boring. Most of the time you just want to get to your final destination so you can begin your experience. And you don't just get into the car without a road map, right? You need to know how to get from point A to point B. I was never much for maps. I have no idea how I got anywhere before we had GPS.

But wouldn't it be more fun if you could enjoy the entire journey as you travel to your destination? Isn't it about the experience? To me it is. If you ask Richard, my sweetheart, he would tell you that my mantra is, "It is all about the experience."

Instead of just renting a car to take us from Vegas to the Grand Canyon, we rented a convertible. We put the top down. We turned on the radio and blasted some great tunes. We didn't just stare straight ahead at the road, we looked around and noticed the changing scenery and vegetation of the desert zones. We even looked up each of the desert zones and learned about them along the way. We noticed blooming cactuses and stopped to take pictures of them. We marveled at the changing shadows of the mountains and stopped at scenic overlooks and took selfies together.

A couple of hours down the road, we stopped on nostalgic Route 66 and stumbled upon a fantastic microbrewery (caution: we brake for microbreweries). We walked the streets and peeked into the local shops. We did a little wine tasting in a local tasting room touting their Arizona wines. We enjoyed our experience.

Once we got to the Grand Canyon, we made our way to the visitor's center and I bought a pink hiking hat for the next day. Because who doesn't need a hot pink hiking hat?

We experienced all of that before we even got to our destination.

Now I know you're here reading a book about how to retire. But, wouldn't you like to enjoy the journey along the way? Aren't you afraid of spending the next ten years toiling and stressing and "working your plan"—are you waiting for the day that you retire before you can enjoy your life? Not me. I want to enjoy every day in my now. If you're familiar with Abraham-Hicks, it's what Abraham refers to as "getting ready to be ready."

Let's get in the car. Right where you are at this moment. Remember, I told you, you're okay exactly where you stand. We're going to get real about where you're starting your journey. We're also going to take some time to figure out exactly where you want to go. Unless you plug that data into your GPS, how are you going to get there?

Once you know where you want to go for your dream destination, you're going to figure out how to get there. You're going to make sure you have enough gas in your tank, you're going to make sure you have enough money to get you there, and you're going to make sure you go the proper speed limit so that you don't get a ticket or worse yet, wreck your car and have to cancel your plans.

And the best and most fun part of all, we're going to make sure you have fun every mile along the way.

I'm going to walk you through my F.R.E.E.D.O.M. process.

Starting where you are right now, we will pull out the map and you will decide where you want to go. We're going to explore your story—and how you feel about money as well as the story you tell yourself and others on a daily basis. Your "I am" is a big indicator of where you are and also where you'll end up.

F: In the first step of my F.R.E.E.D.O.M. process, you're going to learn the importance of putting yourself first.

You're going to learn that "selfish" is not a dirty word. You are going to get real about your relationship with your money by taking a simple assessment that helps you decide where to begin—and you're going to take the first steps in planning, organizing, and gaining control of your finances. And at the end of this chapter, you'll have clarity around your commitment to creating a plan and sticking to it.

R: We're going to discuss risk and reward—in a way that makes sense to you.

We're going to discuss the importance of having clearly articulated goals as well as setting the timeframe for achieving those goals. In addition, we're going to talk about the importance of aligning your goals with your tolerance for risk, and finally, we'll look at some of the most common investment options and the differences between them. By the end of the chapter, you'll have a better understanding of the concept of risk and how it plays a part in your overall strategy.

E: You're going to have the opportunity to look into the future, so that you can begin with the END in mind. This is where you get to plan your dream destination. Yay!

You're going to take some time to dream a little. I'm going to walk you through a visualization exercise that allows you to get lost in dreaming about your deepest desires. You're going to gain insight into what you want your dream retirement to look like. Then, I'm going to walk you through a list of actionable steps you'll need to take in order to have a full understanding of where you currently stand financially and where you would like to be ten to fifteen years down the road.

E: You're going to learn how to plan for emergencies—because life happens.

In this chapter, I will walk you through the importance of having a backup plan in place—a plan to fall back on when life happens. We are going to have the emergency fund discussion, and you are going to learn to create an emergency fund account of your own. You are going to understand why you need one. You're going to know the definition of a true emergency and you'll make a commitment to keep your hands off unless you find yourself in an actual emergency.

D: You're going to learn the value of true diversification. Hang tight and stay with me.

I'm going to teach you a few different types of diversification and the benefits of each. You're going to learn about different kinds of investment accounts and how each of them is taxed, as well as the benefits of having multiple buckets as you plan for retirement. We're also going to discuss the importance of making sure that the investments you hold inside of those accounts are diversified, and finally, I'm going to explain why working with a single financial advisor may benefit you.

O: Oh no. We're going to make sure you don't panic when the market gets noisy.

In this next chapter, I'm going to reveal to you one of the most detrimental and self-sabotaging mistakes you can make. I'm going to shed some light on market volatility (which I refer to as market "noise") so that you are armed with the knowledge necessary to make informed decisions about your money as opposed to allowing yourself to get swept away by your emotions. And you're going to learn about the Rule of 72. By the end of this chapter, you will have strengthened your resolve to stay the course without deviating from your plan.

M: You're going to move it and get going on your journey.

In this final step, you will learn the principles and magic of compounding, and you're going to learn how putting it all together can have an impact on your children and your grandchildren for generations to come.

I've coached many people on the journey you're about to embark on, and I'm so excited that you've made the decision to take ownership of your financial future.

Hop into your convertible and put the top down. Since you're not driving and can't get hurt, pour yourself a glass of wine, and let's go on this road trip together. Can't you almost feel your hair flying free in the wind? Let's have some fun with this. Let's approach the subject of retirement planning in a different way than has ever been done before. Let's be easy with it. Let's be playful. Let's give up all the resistance and stress around the subject and get excited about the possibilities. Let's plan your future and have some fun in your present. Are you ready? Let's go.

Chapter 4:

What's Your Story?

"The only limit to our realization of tomorrow will be our doubts of today."
~ Franklin D. Roosevelt

In this chapter, you're going to take a deep dive into your story and do a little work to identify any limiting beliefs you may have surrounding the subject of money, and by the end of the chapter, you will have identified any beliefs that may be having a negative impact on your financial wellbeing.

Each chapter of my story is unique; some are exciting and beautiful and some are heartbreaking and painful. All of the chapters have led me to the place I am today, which is right here in my living room, snuggled under a blanket, enjoying my coffee, writing this book out of love for you.

There are two types of stories we often tell. One type is our history or biography, which is filled with our life experiences. We have another type of story as well—this is the story we tell ourselves and others on a daily basis and is more like a tape that plays on repeat in a continuous loop inside our head. And most often, this type of story is a result of living through a difficult chapter of life. Can you imagine what it would look like to stop at any point in your life story and say, forget it, I don't like this book; this is where my story ends. When I pulled into my garage so many years ago in my complete and utter desperation, that's exactly what I almost did. But, by the grace of God and the pull of extraordinary universal forces, I got out of that car and continued to walk out my journey. And because I decided to move forward through that yucky chapter, I have so much more to share with the world. And I show up in a completely different way than I would have if I hadn't experienced so much life contrast.

Law of Attraction

You may be familiar with the book, *The Law of Attraction* by Esther and Jerry Hicks. The spiritual concepts are much more mainstream than they were even a few short years ago. The book outlines three irrefutable universal laws: The Law of Attraction, The Law of Deliberate Creating, and the Art of Allowing. If you've somehow been led to pick up this book, I believe you are already a powerful attractor. The Law of Attraction states, "That which is like unto itself is drawn." In essence, you attract what you think about and what you feel.

Have you ever observed someone with what I would call a poverty mentality? Someone who has always struggled financially. It almost seems as if they have a hole in their pocket. Do you have that person in your mind? I'll bet we all know at least one of these people. Now think about the things you hear them say. They talk about their lack of money. They talk about how everyone else has money and they don't. They may even say things like, "the rich get richer and the poor get poorer." They walk around defeated and destitute. And to them, their reality is their truth. They speak of lack and the thought of abundance is so far off of their radar that it doesn't exist for them. They don't have any money to spare and are always counting their pennies. Can you almost sense the vibration they emit? It's so thick you can feel it. It seems as if they live under a dark cloud of poverty.

Most likely you've also observed the complete opposite scenario. We all have friends or acquaintances who ooze wealth. Everything they touch seems to turn to gold. It seems they have more money than they know what to do with, yet you'll rarely hear them talk about money. They certainly aren't worried about it. They're likely having conversations about their experiences, not their money. They are busy finding enjoyment in planning new businesses, taking trips, decorating homes, and living a life of abundance. Can you sense the vibration they're emitting? It has energy, doesn't it? It feels like ease. It feels like freedom. It feels limitless and expansive. It's worth noting that I can feel an elevation in my vibration while I'm writing about their experience of abundance.

I happen to have a friend in this category. Her name is Kimberly. Kim and I met shortly after my first child, Ryan, was born in 1992. I had just divorced and so had she, and we ended up neighbors in my apartment complex. Kim had natural beauty with golden locks and she was beautiful inside and out. She took care of herself by eating clean and was in fantastic shape. Kim was a few years older than me, and I remember being in complete awe of her. She had beautifully decorated her apartment, and it seemed as if she was a natural-born homemaker. I can even remember the smell of fresh linens coming out of her dryer. Why didn't mine smell that way? Everything in her home was immaculate. She loved to cook and enjoyed spending time planting flowers in potted plants outside that she craftily painted herself.

I wanted to be like Kim. Guess what—Kim had been through a divorce and was a single mother, just like me. But she didn't act like it. She was too busy surrounding herself and her daughter with beauty. And she didn't have much money at all. However, she didn't seem worried about it. And sure enough—before I knew it, she was building a successful business with the man she went on to marry. She used her talent to help him build a large internationally renowned clinic—and then she went on to buy a plantation in Georgia where she built a resort business which had always been her dream. She never felt lack; she enjoyed a life of abundance. She surrounded herself with beauty and positivity—as well as a strong belief in God and Universal abundance.

What vibration are you sending out to the Universe? What is the story you tell yourself and others? As I said, we all have a story, and most of us are telling and retelling the same stories day after day. And when we get together for a girl's night out, we tend to repeat the same stories over and over. We even tend to hang out with friends who have similar stories. After a while, we begin to wear our stories like a badge of honor. As humans, we gather together and start clubs where we can commiserate on how terrible our stories are and how wronged we've been—and how we deserve so much more.

And that's okay if your story is the story you want to be living. But if you're not happy with the way your story is playing out, then it's time to stop telling it.

For years, I wore my "single mother/career woman/I'm a martyr" story. It went something like this:

"I am a single mother of five. I've been on my own with five children since 2005. I have an amazing job with *jane iredale* cosmetics. I travel for work and am on a plane every other week, and although I love my job, it's exhausting to do all of it on my own. My son Kyle was born with hypoplastic left heart syndrome, and caring for him has been unbelievably difficult and stressful. I'm tired of doing this on my own and wish I had a good man in my life."

Guess what. I stayed a single mother of five. I suffered from loneliness and exhaustion for many years. I did work hard and I was busy. My life was extremely stressful. Until I stopped telling that story in 2013.

In 2013, I began adding a daily meditation practice into my life. I started journaling every morning and created a vision board. I slowly started learning the art of deliberate creating—and began to gain clarity about what I wanted my life to look like. I stopped telling my sad old story and stopped playing the victim. It was then that my life began to change.

The Vortex

Again, if you're familiar with The Law of Attraction, you're likely familiar with the concept of your Vortex. And there are some of you who may be reading this and saying to yourself *Vortex? What the heck is a Vortex—I thought this was a book about retirement planning.* If you're in this category, hang in here with me, I promise you this is all going to be worth it. Again, I believe you picked up this book for a reason.

The best way I can describe how I envision this Vortex is as a beautiful, magical, swirling funnel that opens up in the atmosphere above me during meditation. The funnel has a small opening at the bottom where there is a point of exit and entry. Inside this swirling mass lives everything I've ever created—all existing magically in a type of vibrational escrow just waiting for the perfect time to make its way through the opening and show up into my now reality in physical form.

The things we've created in our Vortex are created through strong thoughts, feelings and emotions. Abraham explains that when we go through what we would consider negative experiences in our life, we have strong feelings about what we don't want (contrast) and therefore, we shoot up a "rocket of desire" into our Vortex for the exact opposite, which is what we do want.

I have had so many negative or contrasting experiences and feelings in my life that I cannot imagine how many rockets of desire I have sent into my Vortex. I must have millions of dollars in there, just waiting to flow into my experience. I've also got a gorgeous beach house near great SCUBA diving where my future grandchildren run up and down the beach playing in the sand, laughing with their beautiful auburn locks blowing in the warm breeze. I can hear the sound of the seagulls soaring above and can taste the salty air.

Let's test this by thinking about your story.

What is the story you tell about your life? Your health? Your finances? Your relationships? Do you have a story that plays like a tape over and over in your mind and almost torments you on a daily basis?

Before you can begin creating the life you're dreaming of, you need to clean up your vibration and take a good look at your story.

This may be the single most important step you take on your journey, because if you can ease your way into cleaning up your vibration, you can change the trajectory of your entire life.

Blue Paper and Gold Pen Exercise

Now, this exercise can be done without blue paper and a gold pen, but there is something magical about doing it this way. If you're a dreamer, like me, pick up some beautiful blue construction paper and a gold gel pen. I buy mine on Amazon. The darker blue paper works best because the gold shows up better.

Take a regular piece of notebook paper and rip it out so that it has tattered edges.

On this tattered ugly piece of paper, I want you to start writing your story.

What story do you tell about your health and wellness?

What story do you tell yourself and others about your relationships?

What story are you telling yourself about your career? Do you love it? Do you hate it?

What story are you telling about money? (Keep your money story handy for a later chapter.)

Once you've written everything down on this tattered piece of paper, find a quiet space and take fifteen minutes where you won't be disturbed. I am heading to my big comfy brown leather recliner that I use as my meditation chair. I'm going to go make myself a cup of coffee and grab my favorite blanket—I'll meet you there.

Now let's sit in complete stillness for fifteen minutes. I want you to listen for the silence. I like to focus on the hum of the heat or air conditioner, the washing machine or dryer, or even just the sound of the wind outside my window. The key is to let go of all of your thoughts and lose yourself in the silence. Set the intention that you want God or the Universe or whatever is personal to you to help you let go of your old story and help you to find the words to rewrite your new story (but resist the temptation to think your new story into being. This exercise is about letting all of it go and allowing a new story to show itself to you). Imagine that you are entering your Vortex of creation. Inside is a huge storehouse with everything you've ever wanted, thought about, or imagined, and it's all right there waiting to be taken off the shelf. In order to access the keys to this storehouse, you need to quiet your mind and allow your vibration to rise by letting go of all the resistance you hold in your physical body. You are going to connect with your soul—your higher self, your inner-being, your Creator—and it's going to be a delicious and meaningful experience.

Enough talking. Set your alarm, and I'll meet you back here in fifteen minutes.

How did you do? If you're new to meditating, it may have been difficult to clear your mind of thought. Don't stress out about that. It's called a meditation *practice* for a reason. The more often you do it, the easier and more wonderful the experience becomes.

Now it's time to grab your blue paper and gold pen. You're going to write your new story. This is the fun part.

1. Take a piece of your blue paper and have gold pen in hand. Remember, this is magic.
2. Set your alarm for fifteen minutes.
3. For the next fifteen minutes, I want you to start writing your new story. Start by writing anything that comes into your mind. This is your story as you want it to be. Not as things are now—so get creative. Don't let your now reality get in the way.

I'll meet you back here in fifteen minutes. Remember there is something magical about that gold pen. And go.

How did you do? How do you feel? Can you feel a shift in your consciousness and a lift in your vibration? You just took the time to show up for yourself in a new and beautiful way.

We become what we think, what we say, what we do. Thoughts become things. We can be, do, or have anything we want, but our job is to consciously create, think, and then feel wanted things into being. I promise that you will begin to see a shift in your life when you begin changing the story you're telling yourself and others.

If you've been hard on yourself, it's time to stop—it's time to be easy with yourself.

Here is the new story I tell myself every day and sometimes, when no one is around, I speak these things out loud (my dog, Charlie, seems to enjoy it. He even sits on the floor next to me and meditates with me every morning).

I move through my day with effortless ease.
I am love and I am loved.
Every day, in every way, I'm getting better and better
Everything is always working out for me.
I am healthy, I am vibrant, I am a magnetic attractor,
people are drawn to me.
The Universe has my back.
I am right where I need to be.
Money flows freely into my life.

You've likely built up a lot of momentum as a result of telling your current story. Don't be surprised if this takes some time. And your old story may creep back into your thoughts and words for a while. Sometimes old stories pop up after years seemingly out of nowhere for me. When this happens, here's what I do—and what I want you to do as well. I want you to pivot.

Making the Shift

As soon as you realize that an old, unwanted story has shown up in your thoughts, or even worse, you find yourself speaking your unwanted story out loud—example: I can't afford that, I'll never be able to quit this job, I'm exhausted, I feel fat, I hate my thighs—I want you to pivot by learning and practicing the following process.

1. Acknowledge the thought. Don't be hard on yourself— simply observe the thought and acknowledge that it showed up.

2. Immediately choose a better feeling thought. If you cannot find a better feeling thought about that subject, then I want you to change the subject. Stop it in its tracks. Look around you. It could be as simple as noticing the beautiful shade of blue in the sky or the lush green leaves on the trees. If it's a negative thought about the person you're with, then look for one thing you love about that human. That can certainly be tough sometimes, but I guarantee you'll find it, when you purposefully gaze into their soul and search for the good.

3. Remember one thing you wrote down in your new story and repeat it to yourself. Perhaps it's an affirmation like the ones I use for myself.

4. Get on with your day and whatever you do, don't sit and dwell in it. Because when you do that, you're negatively creating more of that!

It may seem simplistic, but it is my absolute promise that when you begin to shift your thinking, you will be able to feel your way into a better feeling state, and your story will begin to write itself in a new way. When you change your story, you change your life.

Now that you've written your new story, I want you to rip up that old, ugly looking paper. And as a declaration to yourself and to the Universe that you are serious about letting it go, I want you to take one more ceremonial step.

1. Create a quiet, sacred space where you won't be interrupted.
2. Light a candle.
3. Say a prayer of thanksgiving for your old story. It has served its purpose and brought you exactly where you are meant to be in this moment. I am one hundred percent certain that your old story has caused you to launch countless rockets of desire—rockets that are about to bring forth incredible manifestations.
4. Once you have given thanks and blessed your story along with all those who have hurt you, I want you to burn the paper, and as it burns, I want you to feel yourself letting all of it go. Imagine your old story disappearing into dust. Making way for the new journey you're about to begin.
5. This is a ritual that I often repeat during a full moon. There is something magical about setting new intentions under the light of the moon. After all, we all have a little witch lying dormant inside of us, don't we? (Wink.)

Great job! You've done some beautiful work here, and you've likely uncovered beliefs that have been limiting your ability to live a life of financial abundance and wellbeing. Now that you have a greater awareness, you have the ability to move forward with intention as you begin to write your next chapter.

Chapter 5:

Live Abundance Now

"If you look at what you have in life, you'll always have more.
If you look at what you don't have in life, you'll never have enough."
~ Oprah Winfrey

In the last chapter, you did some beautiful work on identifying the new story you want to begin writing and creating for yourself. Now, let's take some time to explore practices that will enhance your journey as you begin to write your new chapter.

Remember when we talked about the road trip, and how important it is to enjoy the journey while you're on your way to your new destination? I'm going to share some practices with you that have changed the entire trajectory of my life. I know that your ultimate goal is to experience the retirement of your dreams, and it is my intention that you learn to do just that. However, wouldn't it be lovely if you didn't have to wait ten years before you enjoyed your life? Wouldn't it be amazing to begin living a life of abundance exactly where you are today? No matter what your financial situation, would you like to show up for yourself in a new way beginning today?

Over the last ten years, I have transformed my life by incorporating simple practices into my daily life—these practices have produced manifestations that are worth much more to me than money. They have produced a life that I love; a life of abundance. Abundance comes in many forms. Money is simply a byproduct of abundance. And I would argue that unless you are living a life of abundance before the money shows up, the actual physical currency will not produce the joy you're reaching for.

I want to challenge you to look at abundance in a new way, to view it as a sort of vibrational currency. Are you feeling abundance or lack? If you're feeling lack, we are going to walk through some ways to raise your vibration and bring a feeling of abundance into your life. Right where you stand—in your now reality. If you can raise your vibration, you can tap into your vibrational escrow (Vortex). And when you can tap into your vibrational escrow, the Universe will surprise and delight you in delicious new ways—each new day will continue to get better and better. And soon, instead of feeling depleted and exhausted, you will feel vibrant, alive, energetic, vivacious, and excited about your life.

Now, if you're like me (A-type personality), you may read this chapter and feel like you need to incorporate all of the things I'm about to share with you at once, and you may feel like a failure when you don't do it all perfectly. That is exactly what I have tried to do my entire life. I write my lists and start checking things off. Please don't do that. I'd like you to choose one or two practices that resonate with you and start there. When you do that, you will allow momentum to build and from there, you can attract whatever you're supposed to incorporate next.

Here we go. This is the fun stuff. I can almost feel the hope rising and the vibration of abundance beginning to bubble up.

Meditation

I know that we've already touched on meditation, yet I'm convinced that this is the single most important practice you could incorporate into your daily life. If you only incorporate one new thing, then let it be this one.

I've tried many different ways of meditating through the years and enjoyed all of them. My practice has evolved and continues to evolve. I'm going to share some of my favorite with you here.

Guided meditations are great if you have trouble sitting still and quieting your mind. I used guided meditations for years. My favorite resource is Oprah and Deepak Chopra's 21-Day Meditation Experience. Deepak leads you through twenty-one-days of meditations (fifteen minutes each) on a variety of subjects ranging from health and love to abundance. I love the ritual of marking off a calendar each day for twenty-one days and I think it serves in helping to develop a habit of daily meditation practice.

Another one of my favorite guided meditations is Abraham-Hicks's guided meditations. These can be found by downloading their app. My favorite ones are the *General Wellbeing Meditation* and the *Financial Well Being Meditation*.

Again, these are generally about fifteen minutes long, and I like to do them twice a day, once in the morning and again in the evening before bedtime. I love drifting off to sleep with positive thoughts and feelings of abundance.

For those of you who enjoy or would like to experience mantra meditation, Deva Premal and Miten also offer a powerful 21-day Mantra Meditation Journey that I am also in love with.

For another option, you can download the Insight Timer app for a library of free guided meditations. I haven't used this one much, but my friend Dan Miller—my health guru, International speaker, and all-around cool human—recommends it to his clients.

And finally, Collette Baron Reid has some beautiful guided meditations available by going to her website. While you're there, you can try her daily oracle card reading free for a little added fun.

These days, I've graduated to silent meditation. If you find that silence works better for you, then find a quiet place in your home and do your best to carve out time for yourself, preferably right when you wake up—same time, same place, every day, if possible, is the best practice. You can set a timer if you want to. I usually set mine for an hour. But, fifteen minutes is all you need. Listen for the hum of the heat or air conditioner. If your mind drifts back into thoughts of daily life (and it will), gently, and without judgment, bring your awareness back to the silence. Be easy with it, as if you're lying in bed drifting to sleep. Just allow yourself to be.

I guarantee if you can incorporate the practice of daily meditation ritual into your life, your life will change, and magic will show itself to you in a myriad of ways. Answers to problems will show up out of nowhere. The right people will cross your path. New opportunities will present themselves to you. When you let go of resistance and allow yourself to go with the flow, everything in your experience will look different to you. Please drop me a line to let me know how this goes for you, because I am so excited about the changes that will begin to occur for you almost immediately.

Affirmations

When I first tried to incorporate affirmations into my life, I repeated a few phrases into the mirror as many of the gurus teach you to do. That didn't work for me. Visualize me standing in front of my mirror saying things like *I am healthy, wealthy, and wise. I am thin* (saying this as I'm looking at myself in the mirror with twenty extra pounds on my body). The words fell flat, and I just became irritated by the entire process.

Over the past few years, I have been doing daily affirmations a different way. And this just happened organically, without even thinking about it. One day, as I was exercising on my Peloton bike, I got a burst of energy. My endorphins kicked in. And I started shouting out loud, in my bedroom, while biking:

"Every day in every way, I'm getting better and better. Every day in every way, I'm getting better and better. Every day in every way, I'm getting better and better and stronger and stronger!"

The more I did it, the more my momentum picked up and then other affirmations came into my mind and added to it:

"I am a powerful creator. I am a magnificent attractor! Everything is always working out for me. Abundance flows into my life. I am healthy! I am wealthy. I am wise. I am free! I create the life of my dreams. Money flows into my life. Money flows into my business. I don't know where it comes from, it just flows into my experience. People are drawn to me. I am love and I am loved."

The more momentum I experienced in my physical body, the more momentum I had with my affirmations, and they just flowed out of my mouth. My physical state (the energy of movement) somehow connected with my words, and as a result, I could feel that what I was saying had real power behind it.

I began to realize that this is how thoughts become things, and as a result, powerful creating takes place. When your thoughts are connected to intense feelings and emotions, you are able to energetically raise your vibration. When you can successfully get yourself into a feeling state, your thoughts and words begin to take physical form. You are a powerful creator. A co-creator with God and the Universe. When you can harness this power, anything is possible. If you can imagine it, you can create it. You can be, do, or have anything. The Universe is expansive and abundant.

Now this is also true of things you don't want in your life. We need to watch our words. Have you ever noticed what happens when you argue with someone? The feeling state that you're in when you say harmful words to another person? Couldn't you feel the momentum that occurred when you allowed yourself to get worked up into a state before those words came out? This is something to avoid because in that state, you are negatively creating.

This is why we must pay attention to the story we're telling ourselves and others. Thoughts and words, when connected to feelings, become things. We are always going to receive more of the things we're thinking about and speaking about—whether positive or negative. You are powerful attractors. Pay attention to how you feel. Make it your dominant intention to feel as good as you can. Watch over your words with care. Don't you want more good things? I do. We all do.

The beauty of this affirmation practice is that you're killing two birds with one stone. You can combine this with exercise and it won't take any additional time out of your busy day.

Now, I know some of you may be thinking this sounds like *new age* mumbo jumbo. I don't care what your religious beliefs are, or what your name for God is (God, Source Energy, Spirit, Universal Intelligence), so don't allow yourself to get hung up and stuck here. We are all women. We come in many different colors, shapes and sizes, have diverse backgrounds, and hold different values and spiritual beliefs. My tribe is one of inclusion and diversity. Meditation is just prayer. However, if your prayer consists of begging and pleading instead of knowing and believing, then you may want to take a look at how effective your prayer is. It's not without coincidence that most faiths address the subject of money. And as an example for those of you who still need a little convincing, I'm going to throw in some scripture to back up my point.

"The effectual, fervent prayer of a righteous man availeth much."
– James 5:16, KJV

"Ask and it will be given to you; seek and you will find; knock and the door will be opened to you."
– Matthew 7:7, NIV

"For truly I say to you, that whoever will say to this mountain, be you removed, and be you cast into the sea; and shall not doubt in his heart, but shall believe that those things which he said shall come to pass; he shall have whatever he said."
– Mark 11:23, AKJV

And finally, and I love this one,

"We walk by faith and not by sight."
– 2 Corinthians 5:7, KJV

It's big and important for you to see that you are a deliberate creator, a co-creator with the Universe. This is what you came here for. Artists create exquisite works on canvas, poets write beautiful poems with the ability to make us feel, chefs create delicious cuisine, and writers stimulate new thought by writing down the inspirations whispered into their soul. Photographers have the ability to capture single moments in time. There is so much beauty available for us to tap into, and we aren't even scratching the surface. There is a rich tapestry of life experience available to all of us. When we sit in silence during meditation, in essence, we are allowing ourselves to be still enough to listen to the voice of Spirit. That my friends, is prayer. Meditation is simply prayer. The act of allowing and receiving.

Visualization

Visualization is a bit different from meditation and affirmations and is another powerful process which can be used for creating an extraordinary life.

There are a few different ways that I've done this. One way is to make a vision board. I created a vision board which I keep next to my Peloton bike so that I am able to look at it while I'm riding. I allow the images to help me with my affirmations. I simply took a cork bulletin board and pasted words, phrases, and pictures I cut out of magazines. I cut out images of trips I'd like to take (African safari, wine tasting in Italy), I cut out words that speak to me, like "Powerful," "Vibrant," "Love", and "clean eating." I cut out pictures of healthy meals, fresh fruit, as well as photos of activities I love doing, like SCUBA diving (the Great Barrier Reef in Australia is on my list of future dive sites). Most of the things I cut out represent the feeling or experience I want to have. Of course, I need money to do many of those things, but not all of them. And it is amazing that when I am on my bike, looking at those images, I can almost see, feel, and taste what it is like to experience those things. And again, since I'm visualizing them while I'm exercising, my body is in a physical state of movement. This produces, for me, an energy available for powerful creating.

Thoughts to things. Do you see a pattern here?

Another technique I've used is to sit down and journal or write. Sometimes in the morning after I meditate (most of the time, I do this on Saturday mornings), I will take fifteen minutes to journal. I just write, "What I want to bring into my experience." This is a powerful exercise. Sometimes it's amazing what comes out of it. I write for fifteen minutes and let the words flow onto the paper. This exercise can be especially powerful after coming out of meditation. Try it. You'll be surprised when your inner being shows up and speaks to you.

And finally, if you enjoy visualization techniques and want more, you can find a powerful process described in the book, *The Law of Attraction* by Abraham-Hicks called "the workshop."

Exercise and Move Your Body

I'm not going to say much about exercise because we all know we should do this. What I will say is that part of showing up for yourself is making the time to move your body at least thirty minutes each day. This was a major area of struggle for me until the last couple of years. I dislike the word "exercise." But I will tell you that I love the word "experience," and the word "movement" seems to have a positive vibe to it, too.

Is there anything you've always wanted to do? Over the last few years, I have started to do things I have never done before. I have begun to enjoy the "experience" of fitness. Let me explain.

I have always been a bit of a mermaid in the water, and always wanted to learn to SCUBA dive. A few years ago, I made the decision to get SCUBA certified, and it has been a life-changing event. I feel like a real-life mermaid when I am underwater. In my underwater world, I am completely free. Life under the sea is indescribably beautiful, and the peace that comes from floating alongside marine life and listening to nothing but the sound of my own breath through my regulator puts me into a meditative, dream-like state. And guess what—I also end up burning a lot of calories when I dive.

Last year, at forty-eight, I decided I wanted to become a runner. I had never run a day in my life—not even in high school. I would always look at people running on the street and think to myself, "I wish I could do that." Last year, I decided that I am a runner. I downloaded the Couch to 5k (C25K) app on my phone and began the eight-week C25K program. I started in week one only able to run sixty seconds at a time. Eight weeks later, I ran a full 5K. In fact, at the beginning of the eight-week training, I decided to sign myself up for my first full 5K so that I had something to work toward. I signed up for the Color Run in Minneapolis with my daughter, Cori Lynn. Remember, for me, it is all about the experience. No boring runs for me. Bring out the tutus and fun costumes and throw rainbows of paint on me while I run past in all my glory. After all, I need to celebrate. I am a runner! Side note: I used to say things like "the only time you'll catch me running is if I am being chased by a bear." Did you notice my new story? "I am a runner!"—Why yes, I am.

Not only did I run the Color Run 5K at the end of that eight weeks, I have run four more races since. And I enjoy running a few times a week now. I am pretty slow, but I'm almost fifty years old, and I'm running 5Ks for the first time in my life. That's pretty cool, don't you think?

This year, my sweetheart and I began running together after work and then sitting in the sauna afterward. We decided to replace cocktails and heavy dinners with clean eating and healthy activities. Not only was it more fun for us, we also got into better shape. As a result, we decided to hire a guide and conquered our first hike on the South Rim of the Grand Canyon. What an exhilarating experience. Like I said, it is all about the experience.

Do you have some goal you want to set for yourself? Something to work toward instead of just saying you need to "exercise" every day? If so, you've got this. We've got this. Let's replace the word exercise once and for all and let's use the word experience in its place.

Today, I'm going to enjoy the experience of moving my body. Bam.

Feed Your Mind

This one is easy. What are you feeding your mind? Each day, try to read or listen to something that stimulates your mind and feeds your soul. If you're a reader, then feed your mind by reading a couple chapters a day in a book that not only interests you, but that expands your mind and stimulates new positive thought processes.

If you're not a reader, then I want you download Audible onto your phone today or begin listening to podcasts. I listen to books on Audible every morning in my bathroom while I get ready for work, and then again on the way to work once I get into my car. I love my morning ritual. I bring my coffee and my Bose speaker into the bathroom and feed my mind before my day even begins. That is my time. It's sacred. And again, did you notice that it doesn't take any additional time out of my day to do it, since I'm combining it with getting myself ready for the day? Easy button.

I think I have probably listened to *The Law of Attraction* over 100 times in the past few years while putting on my makeup, and the result has been life-changing for me.

Clean Eating

I am nowhere near where I want to be with this one. I'm sure you're doing way better than I am in this area, but I do want to share a couple of resources that have helped me on my journey toward living a healthier lifestyle.

First and foremost, look up my friend Dan Miller and join his thirty-day challenge on Facebook. When you sign up, he gives you everything you need in order to be successful in this area—and he keeps it simple. He gets paid thousands of dollars to speak to humans all over the globe. He's the real deal. No nonsense. Just a cool guy with a great vibe and a desire to help humans live healthier lives. Go to www.danmillerwellness.com and tell him Debbie sent you.

Here's another hack I use. I try to shop only the outside perimeter of the grocery store. Have you ever noticed that the healthiest foods are on the outer walls of the store and that the interior aisles are filled with highly processed and preserved junk foods?

Dan teaches to focus on eating single-ingredient foods. If you can catch it, kill it, or grow it, you can it eat it. He says to stay away from anything that comes in a box or a bag. If there are ten ingredients on the label—we probably don't want to put that into our bodies.

If you don't have time to cook, you may want to join a healthy meal plan like Pete's Paleo.

I buy these meals and eat them for lunch and dinner when I'm too busy to cook, which is often! Otherwise, I get so hungry by the end of the day that I end up eating junk food.

As I said, I am still a work in progress on this one, so that is the end of my preaching. In fact, I'm preaching to myself as I'm writing this (I just grabbed some raspberries out of the refrigerator and a glass of water).

I find that when I eat as clean as possible and drink clean, pure water on a consistent basis, my mind is clear and I have better connection of mind, body and spirit—as well as more energy.

One more thing: if you have trouble drinking enough water, make it an enjoyable experience. I drink my water out of beautiful wine glasses—it seems to taste better, and it makes me visually happy. Pop a colorful slice of orange, lemon, or lime into it and you're on your way to a more beautiful, hydrated you.

Create a Sacred Space

The final thing I want to talk about here is something that I've found is vital to my feeling of emotional wellbeing. If you're like me, then your surroundings are extremely important to you. In fact, my surroundings have a huge impact on the way I feel. I will even go so far as to say that when I'm feeling out of balance and disconnected, it is usually because I haven't taken the time to pay attention to my surroundings.

Is your home a beautiful and sacred space where you can find sanctuary from the outside world? Or is your home in a state of chaos?

It's not important that you fill your home with expensive furnishings and décor. What's important is that you surround yourself with things that make you feel good. I don't know what that is for you, but I will share what gives me comfort and peace in my home.

First and foremost, if my house is a mess (especially if my kitchen is a mess), it has a negative impact on my overall attitude and state of wellbeing.

Your bedroom should be your private sanctuary. Is your sanctuary clean and organized? Do you love your bed? Is it comfortable? Are your sheets clean? Are they soft and cozy? Is your closet organized? Or does it look like a bomb went off in there?

When I'm feeling like my life is in chaos or I'm feeling a bit out of control, one of the first things I look at is my bedroom. It may be time to spend the weekend organizing your closet and washing your linens. I will share something with you that makes me love my closet—I threw away all of my old plastic hangers and purchased wooden hangers from Target. Now all of my clothes hang nicely (I even hung them in a color-coordinated fashion). There goes my perfectionism again.

Next, take a look at your bed linens. If they're old, worn, or torn, treat yourself to a beautiful, soft new set of sheets. Going to sleep on fresh, new linens will do wonders for your state of wellbeing. You are taking care of everyone else all day. At night, you should be able to rest and recharge in a beautiful, clean, and sacred space of your own.

And finally, is your kitchen sink clean? There is something that affects me psychologically in my kitchen. If my sink is full of dirty dishes, my brain feels messy and cluttered.

I make sure that, every night before I go to sleep, my kitchen sink is clean and shiny. And when I wake up, I make my bed. Simple life hacks that make an enormous difference for me.

How Is Your Self-Care?

Self-care doesn't have to mean going to a day spa for a facial, massage, mani, and pedi. Of course, if you have the time and extra money to take care of yourself in that way, then do that. Remember, I used to own a day spa. I fully subscribe to that way of taking care of myself when I have the time.

But there are some other simple ways in which I love and care for myself on a daily basis, and when life gets difficult or I've had a bad day, especially if I start to feel fatigue and exhaustion begin to creep in, I can usually pull myself out of it by getting back to the basics and incorporating a couple of these rituals into my experience.

Hopefully one or more of these will work for you.

Back to basics: take a bath. Shave your legs. Wash your hair. These things immediately make me feel better.

Light a candle. Play your favorite music on Pandora while you pick up the house. Add essential oil to a diffuser. Splurge on yourself with a bouquet of flowers as a reward for going to the grocery store and put them into a beautiful vase on your kitchen counter. Buy a new plant in a pretty pot, and put it on your windowsill (there is something about a plant that adds life and positive energy + oxygen to your space). Wrap yourself in soft, cozy blankets and have them sitting on the furniture in your home. Turn on your beautiful lamps during the daytime while home enjoying your space. Set out a bowl of fresh fruit for your family (I always feel like such a good mother when I set out a bowl of fresh fruit). Go outside and feel the warmth of the sun, watch the clouds roll by, or sit outside in the evening just to watch the sunset. Go for a short walk and pay attention to the birds and the trees.

When you feel a lack of abundance in your life, try to bring your attention back to the basics and focus on your five senses—sight, hearing, taste, smell, and touch.

In this chapter, I've introduced you to practices that can easily be incorporated into your daily life and I believe that even making small, simple changes to your routine can have a big impact and help you begin living a life of abundance in your now. What is the one thing you'd like to begin doing that has the potential to make the biggest difference for you in this day right where you stand?

I'd like to encourage you to show up for yourself in a new, different, and beautiful way. When you do, I guarantee you will begin to feel the feelings of abundance, and when you feel those feelings on a consistent basis, they will build *momentum* and when you've got enough momentum built, that momentum can move mountains.

Remember, it all begins with a thought. Then a feeling.

Thoughts + feelings = things

When you are able to raise your vibration by creating simple, daily rituals for yourself that help you to feel good *in your now*, you begin to think more positive thoughts. And those thoughts lead to the feeling you're searching for—the feeling of abundance.

"Every day, in every way, I'm getting better and stronger"—and so are you!

Chapter 6:

Show Me the Money

"Everything is unfolding perfectly, and as you relax and find ease in your attitude of trust knowing that well-being is your birth-right, amazing things will happen. Things the likes of which you have not seen before."

~ Abraham-Hicks

You've done a lot of work in the previous chapters and most of it had to do with learning to live a life of abundance, little of it had to do with money itself.

In this chapter, we're going to spend some time talking about money. How you feel about money is personal to you and is typically a result of past experiences and upbringing.

I'm sure you've noticed that some people look like they have a lot of money and some people look like they have little. There are people who spend money they don't have to buy things that make them feel good. And there are people who have millions who never spend a dime more than they have to.

What does money mean to you? What will it buy you that you don't have? How do you feel about having money? Do you have a money story? Do you have fear of not having enough money? Do those fears creep into your experience and rob you of your joy? Or are you easy with your thoughts surrounding money?

In order to move forward, we need to get clear about what money means to you and the relationship you have with your money. Is it a healthy relationship or is it a toxic one?

Money Matters Exercise

Take a few minutes to sit and think about the following questions and then write down whatever comes to your mind.

1. What did your parents teach you about money?
2. Did your parents have a money story? If so, can you hear it right now? Is it the same story you tell yourself? Has it been passed down to you, and are you passing it onto your children?

    Example: Money is the root of all evil, or the only way you can have money is by working hard, unless you were born into a wealthy family.
3. If you have a family story, has it had an impact on your relationship with money?
4. What fears do you have surrounding the subject of money?
5. What do you think of people who have money?
6. What do you think of people who don't have money? Does it define who they are? What are your thoughts or judgments toward them?
7. Is there a perpetual thought that you think about your money? Bills? Ability to earn or manifest money?

Example: I have to be born or marry someone wealthy or win the lottery.

8. What is the story you tell yourself about money? (We did some work on this in an earlier chapter) Is it a story of poverty and lack? Or is it a story of abundance?

9. Do you have a new money story you'd like to tell? If so, write it down.

Now that you've taken the time to reflect on those questions, and you've written down your new money story, I want you to do something even more important. Dream.

Dreaming Exercise

It's time to get quiet again for fifteen minutes.

I want you to sit in a comfortable space, close your eyes, and do a little daydreaming.

What's your biggest money dream or desire? Allow your imagination to run wild.

Imagine you have an unlimited supply of money.

Perhaps you land your dream job. What would that be?

What would you buy, if you could buy anything without concern for cost?

Where would you travel if you could go anywhere in the world?

Who would you travel with?

Perhaps you've won millions in the lottery or come into an incredible inheritance and you have an endless supply of money. Now what?

Be creative. I want you to use your five senses (in your mind's eye).

I want you to see it, taste it, smell it, touch it, and feel it. All of it.

Set a timer and meet me back here in fifteen minutes.

Good. You're back. How did that go? Wow! You are a powerful creator. Good job.

Now let's take a few minutes to identify and write down the feelings you felt from the pretend experience of having everything you've ever dreamt of.

Write down ten feelings you felt during that visualization exercise?

I want to share with you the feelings that came up for me here.

1. It feels effortless.
2. It feels like ease. It feels easy.
3. It feels free.
4. It feels like abundance.
5. It feels limitless.
6. It feels creative.
7. It feels like energy. Boundless energy.
8. It feels like wellbeing.
9. It feels vibrant and shiny.
10. It feels delicious.
11. It feels satisfying.
12. It feels like power. Powerful.
13. It feels like F.R.E.E.D.O.M.

Now you've identified the feelings you felt when you had all of the money you've ever wanted in your hot little hands. Would you agree that even if you're not happy with the amount of money currently held in your checking account, there are people, places, and things in your life that make you feel those same good feeling thoughts you felt during that exercise? I'm willing to bet there are things and people in your life that bring you satisfaction, ease, and joy.

Take a moment now to identify five people, places, or things that make you feel those same feelings you experienced during your visualization exercise:

Oftentimes, we are waiting for more money, a better relationship, a better house, a new car—all so that we can feel the feeling it will give us when we get that thing.

If you can learn to harness the knowledge that you already have the ability to feel those feelings even before you receive the money, the car, the house (all the things you desire) then you can reach for better feeling thoughts right where you are in your now.

The next time you feel stress or fear around the subject of money, bills, debt, or you're getting impatient for the day you'll be able to quit your job and retire, I want you to come back to this exercise and do one of the five things you just listed. I want you to bring to your remembrance the people, places, and things that bring you happiness in your now reality—and begin to reach for those better feeling thoughts. Don't allow yourself to sit in fear or stress for long—simply notice the fear, then decide to pivot, and if all else fails—go meditate or take a nap.

The first step to bringing in the money you desire is to feel the feeling that it will bring you before it manifests in your experience.

Nice job! Over the last few chapters you've done a lot of what I would call inner work—you've dug into your core beliefs about money and may have been a bit surprised by what you discovered along the way. You've also made the brave decision to change any thoughts or beliefs that may have been holding you back from the life of abundance you desire. Now that you've done the inner work, you will turn your attention to creating your new financial plan. Over the next seven chapters, we will walk through seven simple steps that will set you on the path to the financial F.R.E.E.D.O.M. you've been dreaming of.

Chapter 7:

Selfish Is Not a Dirty Word

"Put on your own oxygen mask before assisting others."
~ Randy Pausch

I know the word "selfish" sounds terrible, but it is imperative that you gain a full understanding of this concept. I will walk you through some staggering statistics involving women and their relationship with money, which may surprise you. I'm also going to ask you to take a close look at how well you know your financial situation. And finally, I'm going to ask you to make a commitment to yourself. Let's dive in.

As a woman, one of the first steps necessary to achieving financial freedom oftentimes ends up being much more difficult than it is for men.

As women, we are brought up to be caretakers. We give to everyone around us and sacrifice parts of ourselves and have somehow learned to wear that as a badge of honor. But how is it benefiting anyone around us when we neglect taking care of ourselves in the name of love? Here are a few staggering realities:

- Women tend to live longer than men. This means that we also live longer in retirement and in return, we need our money to last longer.

- Women often have spent fewer years in the workforce. We've taken time off to raise our children and perhaps even care for our aging parents. This means we have less saved for retirement than our male counterparts (and we are living longer).

- The average age of widows in the U.S. today is fifty-six. (U.S. Census Bureau)

- When women are widowed, income is reduced by fifty percent while expenses only drop by twenty percent. (The Hartford, Why Women Worry Study, 2007)

- Due to less time in the workforce, the average monthly Social Security payment to retired women is eighty-seven percent of that paid to men. ("Women Need Advisors, Annuities for Retirement" by Donna Mitchell, financialplanning.com, Feb. 3, 2011.)

Those are some scary stats. However, did you know?

- Women control or influence almost $25 trillion of U.S. household assets. (Hearts and Wallets, "10 Things to Know about Women and Investing," 2014.)

- Forty percent of women report being the family breadwinner.

- One-third of working wives earn more than their husbands.

- As of 2014, there were about 9.1 million women-owned business in the U.S. generating $1.4 trillion of revenue. (American Express. "The 2014 State of Women-Owned Businesses Report." 2014.)

We've been earning more and gaining more spending power over the past few decades and slowly beginning to take control of our financial future. While we've made great strides, we are still not comfortable and confident making investment decisions, and most of us have never consulted with a financial advisor to see how it could help us to feel more confident, informed, in control, and secure.

For women, the financial devastation of death and divorce can be tragic. Let me tell you about my friend Kate. Kate was married to Ben for twenty-six years. Both of them had great jobs, he was a Senior Executive with a large investment firm, and she worked as an interior decorator. Kate and Ben had two small children and seemed like the perfect couple—I remember even feeling a bit jealous of their seemingly perfect lives. The kids were always involved in sports, and Kate was constantly on the go. They were both fit and gorgeous and had a fantastic social network of friends. They owned a beautiful home near the beach, had their kids in private schools. It seemed like Kate had everything a girl could ask for.

One afternoon, Ben went for a run and dropped dead of a heart attack at fifty-two. I watched Kate's world collapse around her. Not only had her sweetheart just died and left her alone to care for their children, but Kate knew nothing about their financial situation. Ben handled all of their bills, investments, and taxes. She didn't know where any of their important documents were kept, she had no idea if they had any life insurance policies, and, if it wasn't bad enough that her husband had passed away, she was now without his income and had no idea if she was going to be okay and able to live the lifestyle that she and her children were used to living. She was grieving and terrified.

It is bad enough to lose a spouse to divorce or death, but throw on top of that the financial stress of not having an intimate relationship with your finances.

The fact that you picked up this book tells me that you're thinking about getting serious. If so, I want you to take a good look at your finances. It's time to get into an intimate relationship with your spending and saving. This is what putting yourself first looks like.

In order for you to do that, you need to understand where you are today.

I want you to answer true or false to each of these questions:

1. I know how much money I/we spend each month (mortgage, utilities, food, clothing, education, insurance, entertainment).

2. I know the location and amounts of all of my/our investments (cash, CDs, stocks, bonds, mutual funds, and real estate).

3. I/We have saved six months' worth of living expenses (think about the gross amount spent on a six-month basis).

4. I know the rate of return each year for each of my/our investments (include the rate of return for CDs, stocks, bonds, mutual funds, real estate, and other investments).

5. I know how much I am/we are saving for retirement (note if this is a regular monthly amount and/or if you use systematic investing).

6. I know the value and location of all of my/our retirement accounts (think about employer-sponsored plans, IRAs, and annuities).

7. I know how much I am/we are estimated to get from Social Security (you can find your statement and also estimate your benefits online at: www.ssa.gov).

8. I know how much insurance coverage I/we have (hink about life, disability, and long-term care coverage).

9. I know how much debt I owe and what percent of interest rate I'm being charged for each debt.

How did you do? The more statements you marked true, the better you know your financial situation.

For any questions that you marked false, I want you to make a commitment to learning the answers before you move forward to the next step.

As I confessed to you earlier, before becoming a financial professional, I had no idea how to handle my finances and knew less than nothing about investing, investments, and how to plan for my retirement. The only thing I did right during those years was to invest the max into my 401K plan at work. Somehow, I innately understood that I needed to pay myself first and put money away for retirement. Not only did I want the company match, I think I knew that I had better sock as much into that plan as I possibly could, especially given the fact that I was a single woman without anyone else to rely on. Thankfully, I did. The act of maxing out my 401k retirement plan and my commitment to continuing to do so over the next ten years, combined with the other aspects of my plan, will ensure that I am able to live the life I'm dreaming of in retirement (I can already hear the ocean waves crashing against the shore in front of my dream beach house).

How about you? Have you been contributing just enough to get your company match? Or have you been focusing on maxing out your plan each year?

Contributions Limits in 2019

The current 2019 401K contribution limits are $19K with a catch-up contribution of $6K for those fifty and over.

In addition to making contributions to your employer retirement plan, you are also eligible to make annual contributions to an IRA (Individual Retirement Plan) each year. Contribution limits for an IRA and ROTH IRA are $6K with an annual catch-up contribution of $1K for those fifty and over.

Over the next couple of chapters, we are going to dig in deeper and it will require real commitment on your part. Are you ready to make a change and then commit to sticking to it? That's what powerful women do. You've got this!

Step 1

I want you to begin by purchasing a three-ring binder which you will use to hold all of your financial information and important documents. Work your way through those questions again and begin to gather all of the information and documents in one place.

Step 2

If you are not contributing the max to your 401K or employer retirement plan, sit down and figure out how much more you can afford to contribute. Don't delay. This may mean cutting your spending. Are you willing to do that?

Note: If you have credit card debt, I want you to pay that off first. Make a list of creditors, the amount owed to each, and the interest rate being charged to you. Make a plan to get out of debt now.

Here are a few tips to get you started:

1. Call your credit card company and ask for a lower interest rate.
2. Consider transferring your balance to a low interest rate credit card.
3. Begin either by paying smaller debts first or by tackling the card with the highest interest rate.
4. Cut your monthly spending until you're out of debt.
5. Pay as much as you can so you're paying more than just the interest each month.

It's imperative you take a good look at your credit card statements. If you are strictly making the minimum monthly payments on anything above an introductory rate 0% card, then you're paying interest on your balance. In many cases, the interest is as high as 18% to 24%. Virtually no investment will give you returns to match an 18% interest rate on your credit card.

In addition to the financial impact of carrying too much debt, the resulting stress can have a detrimental effect on your mental and physical wellbeing. The cumulative effect of carrying credit card debt can be devastating. Remember this the next time you have an impulse to hand over the plastic: Nothing is on sale when you use a credit card without the intention to pay it off in full each month.

Step 3

I want you to commit to putting yourself first. It's time to be selfish.

It's time to put your own oxygen mask on. If you don't have a solid plan for your financial future and aren't on track to retire comfortably, then from this day forward, you can no longer give financial assistance to any child, family member, or friend.

How in the world will you be able to save anyone else if you're struggling? In fact, at some point in the future, you will be asking your children for help if you don't have a solid and successful plan in place.

When you have a solid investment plan in place, your money should last longer than you do, and will not only help your children, but it may also help your family for generations to come. Is that selfish?

It's time to make a decision. What is F.R.E.E.D.O.M. worth to you?

- I'd like you to take a few minutes to write down in a sentence or two what commitment you are willing to make to yourself, beginning today.
- How are you willing to show up differently for yourself and your family?
- I want you to be one hundred percent committed to paying yourself first.

- And I want you to teach this to your children and your grandchildren.

In this chapter, you've begun to set the foundation for your plan. You've heard the adage, knowledge is power. It is power!

You now understand that getting intimate with your money and taking ownership of your financial situation isn't just a nice thing to do—it is essential. By now, my hope is that you've made the commitment to be selfish, and that you also have an understanding that being selfish in this way is one of the most selfless things you can do. When you make the decision to take care of yourself, you set a good example for those who are watching. No longer will you bury your head in the sand because money "isn't your thing." No longer will you financially enable your children or anyone else around you. You will now take ownership of your finances, and your future self will thank you for it.

There is freedom in your future; can you feel it?

Chapter 8:

Risk and Reward

"Whether we're talking about socks or stocks, I like buying quality merchandise when it is marked down."
~ Warren Buffet

It's time to discuss the importance of having clearly articulated goals and setting the timeframe for achieving those goals. In addition, we're going to talk about aligning your goals with your tolerance for risk, and then we'll look at some investment options and the differences between them. By the end of this chapter, you'll have a better understanding of the concept of risk and how it plays a part in your overall strategy.

Before you begin putting together your plan, it's important for you to understand your tolerance for risk and market volatility.

In addition, it is important that you have a clearly articulated goal, which in this case is your dream retirement, and it's also important that you set a timeline for how long you have in order to achieve your goal. Remember the dreaming exercise we did? Get as specific as you can when you're setting your dream retirement goal. Where will you live? How much will it cost you? What activities will you enjoy doing? Your spending habits may change, and it's important to capture that information when you're in the process of setting your goal.

Until you have all of that information available to you and a true understanding of your situation, both now and in the future, you will not be able to determine the right mix of investment vehicles to get you where you want to be.

Knowing how you may react to the ups and downs of the market is also important, because too often, your reactions to swings in your portfolio value, not the fluctuations themselves, have the biggest impact on successfully achieving your goals.

My friend Jill panics every single time she gets her monthly investment statement. She gets completely wrapped up in the nightly news reports and frequently calls from Florida to tell me she is thinking of pulling all of her money out of her investments because we're on the "verge of a recession." She's said this for the past three years—all the while, the market continued to climb higher and higher. She is terrified of losing a dime in her portfolio. She's forty-five years old and still has at least fifteen to twenty years before she will need a dime of her money.

However, it is important to note that, no matter how much she knows or how well educated she is about market movement, she is never going to feel comfortable. That is just how she is wired. I'm saying this to you because investing is not a one size fits all dress. It's more like a little black dress—it's specific to each individual. It wouldn't be good for Jill to be stressed out and frazzled every day for the next twenty years, would it? Her tolerance for risk, or lack thereof, may mean that she chooses a more conservative approach to investing which for her may result in living a more stress-free life.

My friend Suzanne is completely the opposite. She realizes that the market fluctuates constantly, and she is always chasing the higher yield. She is constantly on the lookout for the hottest new stock picks and wants only the best performing funds in her portfolio. Unfortunately, by the time the hottest, best performing investments are on her radar, they are selling close to their fifty-two-week high because everyone else is also buying them. Is that the time to buy? Would she be better off to think about buying low and selling high? And more importantly, she may want to choose the right mix of investments for her goal and make the decision to stay the course.

Before you go any further, let's discuss the concept of risk.

Investopedia breaks down risk tolerance into three categories. This should help you to identify where you fall on the spectrum.

Aggressive Risk Tolerance

Aggressive investors tend to be market-savvy. A deep understanding of securities (including stocks, mutual funds, and ETF's) and the way they work allows such individuals to purchase highly volatile instruments, such as small-company stocks. Aggressive investors reach for maximum returns with maximum risk.

Note: there is a middle ground between aggressive and moderate.

Moderate Risk Tolerance

Moderate investors accept some risk to principal, but adopt a balanced approach with intermediate-term time horizons of five to ten years. Combining large-company mutual funds with less volatile bonds and riskless securities, moderate investors often pursue a 50/50 structure. A typical strategy might involve investing half of the portfolio in a dividend-paying, growth fund.

Note: There is a middle ground between conservative and moderate.

Conservative Risk Tolerance

Conservative investors are willing to accept little to no volatility in their investment portfolios. Often, retirees who have spent decades building a nest egg are unwilling to allow any type of risk to their principal. A conservative investor targets investment vehicles that are guaranteed and highly liquid. Risk-averse (more conservative) individuals opt for bank certificates of deposit (CDs), money markets, or U.S. Treasuries for income and preservation of capital.

These definitions are pretty black and white, so please be aware that your portfolio should be customized to fit your unique situation and objectives.

After determining your comfort with risk, it is important to align it with your goals, time horizon, and expected return in order to help develop your investment strategy, making adjustments over time as needed. A clear understanding of these can help you avoid what may be the biggest risk of all: not achieving your dream retirement goal.

A good financial advisor can add a lot of value and take the angst out of investing on your own; however, even if you choose to seek help with your portfolio, I want you to continue moving forward through these steps so that you are fully involved in the process of creating your plan.

Recap:

1. Identify your goal. What is the exact amount you will need in order to achieve your goal?

2. Identify your tolerance for risk (aggressive, moderately aggressive, moderate, conservative or somewhere in between).

3. Identify your timeline. How long do you have in order to achieve your financial goal?

Why is this important? If you had a short timeframe for achieving your goal, and you knew you needed most of the money in your account within the next year or so, you may want your money in something liquid and conservative such as short term CDs or Money Market instruments instead of having your money tied up in investments that would fluctuate in value with the market.

Whereas, if you had ten years before you'd need your money, you would have more time to allow it to grow and may be better served by investing in quality, long-term equity investments such as stocks, mutual funds, or ETFs.

Most 401K plans today have a variety of mutual funds to choose from, and in addition, most of them offer Target Date funds. These funds typically rebalance to a more conservative mix of investments the closer you get to your retirement date.

Let's go through a few basics that I think every man, woman, and teenager needs to know.

With investments, you either own or you loan. Let's take a look at the Investopedia definitions of each.

Own It

What Is a Stock?

A stock (also known as "shares" or "equity") is a type of security that signifies proportionate ownership in the issuing corporation. This entitles the stockholder to that proportion of the corporation's assets and earnings.

Stocks are bought and sold predominantly on stock exchanges and are the foundation of nearly every portfolio. These transactions have to conform to government regulations, which are meant to protect investors from fraudulent practices. Historically, they have outperformed most other investments over the long run.

What Is a Mutual Fund?

A mutual fund is a type of financial vehicle made up of a pool of money collected from many investors to invest in securities such as stocks, bonds, money market instruments, and other assets

Mutual funds give small or individual investors access to professionally managed portfolios of equities, bonds, and other securities. Each shareholder, therefore, participates proportionally in the gains or losses of the fund.

Loan It

What Is a Bond?

A bond is a fixed income instrument that represents a loan made by an investor to a borrower (typically corporate or governmental). A bond could be thought of as an I.O.U. between the lender and borrower that includes the details of the loan and its payments. Bonds are used by companies, municipalities, states, and sovereign governments to finance projects and operations. Owners of bonds are debtholders, or creditors, of the issuer. Bond details include the end date when the principal of the loan is due to be paid to the bond owner and usually includes the terms variable or fixed interest payments made by the borrower.

What Is a CD?

A certificate of deposit (CD) is a savings certificate with a fixed maturity date and specified fixed interest rate that can be issued in any denomination aside from minimum investment requirements. A CD restricts access to the funds until the maturity date of the investment. CDs are generally issued by commercial banks and are insured by the Federal Deposit Insurance Corporation (FDIC) up to $250,000 per individual.

Note: Most well-diversified portfolios will contain a mixture of these investments depending on the risk tolerance and timeline associated with the goal.

I should briefly mention risk in a way that may not have occurred to you. What is the risk of not investing? Even though it may seem like there is no risk in putting all of your money under your mattress or keeping it in a savings account or checking account, the risk of doing that, in my opinion, is much greater. The risk is that your money will not go to work for you.

In Chapter 12, we will take a deeper dive into a concept that will put that into perspective for you, called the Rule of 72.

There is only one thing that I will guarantee you when it comes to investing: the market fluctuates daily and your investment value will go up and down. Your statements will therefore fluctuate up and down. And when we discuss market volatility later in Chapter 12, my hope is that you will learn to get excited when that happens. Why? Because if you're not planning to retire for another ten to fifteen years, you still have time on your side.

In this chapter, we discussed the importance of having clearly articulated goals and the importance of setting the timeframe for achieving those goals. In addition, we talked about the importance of aligning your goals with your tolerance for risk. We looked at some basic investment options and the differences between them. With that being said, you cannot create a strategy without having a clearly defined goal. This is where the real fun begins.

Chapter 9:

Begin with the End in Mind

"The universe knows the perfect timing for all those things you want and will find, through the crack of least resistance, the best way to deliver it to you."

~ Abraham Hicks

In this chapter, you're going to have the opportunity to dream again! Remember, a little earlier when we discussed the importance of having a clear vision of your goals in order to achieve them? I'm going to walk you through another visualization exercise that allows you to get lost in dreaming about your deepest desires. This exercise will help you gain further clarity of your ideal retirement vision. Then, I'm going to walk you through a list of actionable steps you'll need to take in order to begin moving in the right direction. At the end of this chapter, you will know exactly where you stand now as well as what it will take to achieve your goals.

Let's begin with the end in mind.

Where do you envision yourself in ten to fifteen years?

Do you plan on living in the same house and spending more time with your children and grandchildren?

Do you have dreams of lying on a beach somewhere in the Caribbean?

Do you think your spending habits will remain the same?

Will you be spending less (hopefully you will have paid off your home and cars by then)?

Will you still have a mortgage or a car payment? If so, you may be spending about the same amount of money.

Do you think you want to explore and travel the world during retirement? If so, you will probably spend more than you're spending now.

The first thing we need to do here is get a clear picture of what you're spending now, and how much you think you'll be spending when you arrive in retirement.

Dreaming Visualization Exercise

Take five minutes and close your eyes. Allow your imagination to carry you into the future, to a day in your life approximately one month after you've officially retired from your career.

Where are you?

Who are you with?

What are you doing?

What do you have planned for the day?

Look around, what do you see?

What does it smell like?

What do you taste? Are you drinking or eating anything?

What do you hear around you?

What do you feel?

Allow your inner being to take you to the place you've been dreaming of and allow yourself to experience it with all of your senses.

Feel free to journal in this exercise if that's easier for you.

Come on back when you're ready. I'll be waiting.

Wasn't that fun? Did you notice the feelings you felt just by visualizing being in that magical place? The fantastic part is that you can go back there anytime you want—and I encourage you to do that as often as you can. The feeling state of that vision you are holding space for in your mind is powerful, and if you harness it on a regular basis, and use it to replace any of your old negative thoughts and fears, you will begin to create your new vibrational reality—and you'll be able to enjoy it before it even shows up.

Consider this. I'm sure you've heard stories of prisoners in concentration camps who learned to visit beautiful places in their mind and were able to hold a state of wellbeing in the midst of unspeakable horrors. They were able to withstand and overcome the unbearable treatment and intolerable conditions of being held captive. They held on to their faith and learned to raise their vibration and take control of their internal climate. Truly remarkable. They were able to maintain control in a situation in which their physical body was under complete control by a vicious enemy.

How much more are you able to choose happy thoughts? Visualization practice is a powerful tool. Combined with the practice of feeling gratitude for where we are in our now reality, I'm convinced that we have the ability to be, do, or have anything we desire.

When you picked up this book, I assume you were looking for a "how-to" to make sure you're prepared to retire—am I right? Well, it's time to get down to business.

You're going to need a clean space and a couple of hours in order to tackle this project.

You're about to take a huge step toward ownership of your financial future and will feel empowered to move forward to create your new plan.

Things You Will Need

- The three-ring binder we discussed in an earlier chapter, lined paper or a legal pad, (you may even prefer to work in an Excel spreadsheet).
- Pull all of your financial and investment statements together for reference.
- Gather all statements from any debt you owe (credit cards, mortgage, cars, boats, and other loans).
- Gather all of your monthly bills and a record of spending (if you use online bill pay, it may be helpful for you to go back and print off the last six months of spending).

Once you've gathered all of these items, come on back and we'll get started.

If you're married and you're going to include your spouse in your plan, then you'll want to gather all of your combined assets and information, unless you're interested to see where you stand on your own (which is never a bad idea).

Pulling it all together

1. Create a household budget, if you don't already have one.

   Make a list of all of your monthly bills as well as your average spending on other items like clothes and entertainment.

Once you have that number, come on back and we'll continue.

1. Write down your average monthly spending.
2. Write down your average annual spending.

Note: You can find some simple budget worksheets online if you need help in this area.

Great work. That is a huge accomplishment. Now, I want you to do a little more work.

1. Based on your current annual spending, how much do you think you will spend per year when you retire? If you will have paid off your mortgage and eliminated car payments by the time you retire, then you may be spending less. If you plan to travel the world in style, then you may be spending as much, or more than you are now.
2. Best case scenario, in how many years would you like to retire?

3. Now, I want you to pull together all of your investments/ statements and make a list of what you currently have saved for retirement. Any old or current employer plans, 401Ks, IRAs, ROTH IRAs, CDs, savings, and checking accounts.

4. Write down the total of all investment accounts designated for retirement.

5. Now write down the average rate of return on your investments. You should be able to find your average rate of return on your investment statements.

6. Now you're going to take some time to list any debt you owe. I want you to make some calls if you need to. Find out what the loan payoff amounts are as well as the interest rate you're being charged for each. Your list should look something like this:

    • Mortgage: (Example: Loan payoff $280K, Interest: 3.75%, Monthly payment: $2K)
    • Car loan:
    • Credit card one:
    • Credit card two:
    • Other loans:

Important: Remember, if you have credit card debt, I want you to focus on paying it off as the first step in creating your retirement plan.

1. Write down the amount of credit card debt you are one hundred percent committed to paying off and by which date you plan to do it by.

You're almost there.

1. Now I want you to visit www.ssa.gov and pull your Social Security report. How much will your monthly benefit be at full retirement age or even better yet, at age seventy? At age seventy, you will qualify for the largest possible benefit.

Most people don't understand that they can tap into their other investments such as 401K or IRAs while delaying their Social Security benefits until age seventy. Waiting until age seventy buys you more income for the rest of your life.

Write down your Social Security monthly benefit and your spouse's Social Security monthly benefit, if applicable.

1. If you presently work or have worked for an employer who provides a pension plan, and you will receive a monthly benefit, enter that amount here.

2. And finally, do you have longevity in your family? What is your life expectancy?

According to data compiled by Social Security:

- A man reaching age sixty-five today can expect to live, on average, until age eighty-four.
- A woman turning age sixty-five today can expect to live, on average, until eighty-six-and-a-half.

It's important to note that those are just averages. They also cite that about one out of every three sixty-five-year-olds today will live past age ninety, and about one out of seven will live past age ninety-five.

Congratulations. You've just completed your prework. It's time to plug that information into a retirement calculator. You can find a free online calculator at www.AARP.org or just google AARP Retirement Calculator.

1. Take all of the information you just gathered and within minutes, you should have a pretty good idea of how much you need to have saved for retirement. Write down that amount. This is your retirement goal!

How did you do? Are you on track to achieve your goal? If so, pat yourself on the back and keep going.

If not, and you're sitting there in a complete panic, then you have some more work to do. And that's okay. Remember, I told you to come just as you are. No judgment. It just means that you need to get committed to creating an aggressive plan of saving and then stick to your plan at all cost.

Consider your options:

1. Are you willing to spend less? If so, where can you cut spending right now?

2. Are you willing to work longer? Play around with age in the calculator.

3. Are you willing to work part-time doing something you enjoy during retirement? Perhaps offering consulting services?

4. Are you willing to commit to saving more out of every paycheck? If so, how much more do you need to save? Run the numbers again in the calculator.

5. And here is another option, and I am only recommending it because I did this one myself while

working on my own retirement plan—are you willing to downsize your life? Downsize to a less expensive home or car, and/or sell any of your expensive toys?

The most important and valuable takeaway from this exercise is knowledge. You should now have a good understanding of where you are (if you don't know where you are, you will have no idea how to get to where you want to be). Imagine that you are now sitting in your car, about to begin an amazing journey. You are clear about what it is going to take in order to live the retirement of your dreams. Yes, you have clarified your goal. You know where you are headed: your dream destination.

You Are Beginning with the End in Mind.

Now is the perfect time to bring it all together and pull in some of the practices we learned in the first few chapters.

I think it's time for a fifteen-minute meditation break.

Please go back to your sacred space. I am in mine, wearing my comfy, cozy sweats, sitting in my big leather recliner with a large, soft faux fur chocolate blanket and a cup of coffee in hand.

When you're ready, I want you to begin by taking inventory of how you're *feeling* right now after going through that exercise.

Are you feeling anxious? Or empowered? Or maybe a little of both?

Are you feeling hopeful? Or hopeless?

Encouraged? You've got this! Or defeated and feeling like you'll never be able to retire?

No matter what you're feeling in this moment, just acknowledge those feelings. They are here to serve you.

Now I want you to take three deep breaths and release all of those feelings.

I want you to speak kindly to yourself (silently) and begin to speak words of gratitude about where you are in your now. Begin to think about all of the things you're grateful for, right where you stand. Silently list at least ten things you're grateful for and acknowledge how far you've come (you may even want to write them down).

Gratitude

I am willing to bet that you felt your vibration begin to rise while thinking these better-feeling thoughts. Perfect.

Now it's time to sit in silence for fifteen minutes. Just be. Allow yourself to sit in the receiving mode without any expectation. Just sit. Just be. Allow the Universe, God, Your Higher Self, Your Inner Being to bring you to a place of refreshment and reset.

You've got this. You are in the right place, and this is the perfect time. You are loved and supported.

You've done some extraordinary work today. Everyone you know is planning to retire someday, but few women have done the work you've just completed. And I'm not talking about the act of gathering the data and running the numbers in order to come up with a plan. I'm also talking about the dreaming. Most people just work—day in and day out, and somehow one day, they arrive at their retirement date. Once they get there, they have no idea what to do with their time. Do you know anyone like this? I know a lot of folks that fit into this category. Not you—you've begun the work to create the retirement of your dreams. In this chapter, you worked on visualizing all of it—you were able to see it, hear it, taste it, smell it, touch it. And then, you completed the difficult task of not only looking at where you are, but mapping out where you want to be. You have begun with the end in mind. Fabulous!

It's time for a well-deserved break. When we come back, we'll talk about making sure you're prepared for any bumps you may encounter along your journey.

Chapter 10:

What to Do When Life Happens

"Every time you borrow money, you're robbing your future self."
~ Nathan W. Morris

You've figured out where you want to go and what it's going to take to get to your dream destination, and now we need to discuss the importance of having a backup plan in place—a plan to fall back on when life happens. We are going to have the emergency fund discussion. Likely, this has been on your to-do list for about twenty years. If you already have an emergency fund in place, fantastic! However, I want you to read this chapter anyway because we're also going to discuss the one thing I never want you to do to your future self. It is essential to have an emergency fund in place, yet there are many excuses you can come up with for not having one. I'm going to add in an element of fun to make it easier for you. Before this chapter is over, you are going to create your own emergency fund account. You are going to understand why you need one.

You're going to have fun naming your account. And we're going to discuss the definition of a true emergency.

First and foremost, I believe the main reason most of you haven't set money aside in an emergency fund already is that you think the task is too daunting. And, most likely, you never feel you have enough extra money available to put toward such a noble cause.

I'm going to give you permission to start small, but I'm going to ask you to start now.

Think about this for a minute. How did you accumulate money in your 401K or other employer plan at work? You put a small amount aside out of every paycheck, didn't you?

Remember a couple chapters ago when we discussed paying yourself first? This is where the rubber meets the road.

Today—yes that's right, I said today—I want you to open a separate account, either at your bank or with your financial advisor. This cannot be combined with any current checking or savings account. It must be kept separate.

Now, I want you to decide on an amount that you will be able to set aside each month, or out of each paycheck. Can you afford to put away 10% of your paycheck? How much does that equate to? For example, $200. Whatever it is, I want you to sit and think about what else you are spending that $200 on each month that you may be able to eliminate or go without until you've shown up for yourself and taken care of yourself in this way.

It bears repeating once more—if you have outstanding credit card debt, please work on eliminating that first. Once you've eliminated your debt, you can add up all of the monthly minimum payments you've been paying on your credit cards and pay yourself in this new emergency fund account instead. Think how wonderful it will feel to pay yourself instead of your creditors.

You can set up an automatic transfer from your checking account into your new emergency account. It can be weekly, bi-weekly, or monthly, you decide.

In order to keep you accountable to yourself, it's time to write down your commitment.

Emergency Fund

How much will you contribute weekly, bi-weekly, or monthly, and on what date?

Now that you've made the incredible and monumental decision to show up for yourself in a beautiful new way, I want you to have a little fun with this (remember, it's all about the experience).

You get to name your new emergency fund account.

I named mine my F.R.E.E.D.O.M. Account.

How will you feel when you've accumulated six months of living expenses? My guess is that you'll feel free, safe, secure, expansive, and overall proud of yourself.

Go ahead and name it.

Bam. You did it. That's the most difficult part of starting an emergency fund. Just starting it.

Now what? Forget you have it! Do not touch it. Pretend that there is a 100% penalty for touching that money. Because there is. Once you touch it, 100% of what you take out will be gone. And so will your safety net.

Let me define "emergency."

A major medical issue or crisis. The loss of your job or loss of income. A time where you cannot pay your bills for months at a time. Those are the only things that constitute an emergency.

Here are a few tips to help you grow your new F.R.E.E.D.O.M. fund (doesn't that sound good?).

- Consider depositing your annual tax refund into this account until you have it built up.
- Anytime you receive a bonus or some extra money flows into your experience, pop it into that account.

As always, we need a goal. Let's create yours now. What is your net monthly (after tax) income?

Now, take your monthly income and multiply it by six months.

$_____ x 6 = (your F.R.E.E.D.O.M. fund goal)

Note: Ideally, I'd like for you to have eight months of living expenses saved up. You're going to begin with six months as your initial goal.

Remember, you are now selfish, and you must put your own oxygen make on first. This money should never be used to give to a child, relative, or friend in need of bailing out. You are to pretend this money does not exist.

Still not convinced that you need this?

One of the most frustrating and heartbreaking things I have witnessed is people who take large sums of money from their 401K or IRA plan before they've reached the age of fifty-nine-

and-a-half. Not only do they have to pay taxes on the money they withdraw, they also have to pay a 10% penalty for doing so before the age of fifty-nine-and-a-half.

In the past year, I've had three friends who have taken early withdrawals of money from their retirement accounts in order to pay off credit card debt after getting themselves into a bind.

Note: The following story is fictional in order to illustrate what happens when taking early withdrawals from retirement accounts.

Elizabeth had never been married. She lived on her own in downtown Chicago. She had a fantastic job as the head of HR at a local hospital (let's call her Lizzy—she prefers that). Lizzy loved to go out with her girlfriends on the weekends and did a lot of damage shopping on Michigan Avenue. She allowed her spending to get out of control and ended up with approximately $40,000 in credit card debt. She then made the noble decision to turn over a new leaf and get herself out of debt. Great! Her decision to get out of debt was commendable. However, she decided to take from money she had accumulated in her retirement accounts in order to pay off her creditors. Lizzy stole from her future self. And I'm going to use her example to illustrate my point.

Lizzy took a $50,000 withdrawal from her IRA before age fifty-nine-and-a-half.

As a result, the following was withheld for taxes and penalties: Lizzy is in the 24% tax bracket—she may have paid 24% Federal tax, somewhere around 6% State tax, and a 10% penalty for early withdrawal.

Not only did Lizzy take $50,000 out of her retirement account—which will no longer be working for her and compounding over time—she took 40% off the top of that and handed it to Uncle Sam. In her case, $20,000 came right out of that money, leaving only $30,000 of her original $50,000 to use for paying off her credit card debt.

The other thing most people don't think about when making the decision to take an early withdrawal is what happens to the potential future value of their money. In this case, we are illustrating the future value of $50,000.

Before Lizzy's decision to liquidate her investments in order to pay off debt, she earned a 10% average rate of return in her 401K. In this example: $50,000 earning 10% for ten years equals $129,704.

If you ever want to play around with this type of example, you can google Future Value of Money Calculators and plug in your own numbers.

Using Lizzy's example, she withdrew $50,000 from her IRA, received $30,000 to pay off credit card debt, handed 40% of her hard-earned money to Uncle Sam (a whopping total of $20,000), and gave up the probability of having her money grow to almost $130,000 at the end of ten years.

Let's take this one step further. How long did that $50,000 withdrawal set her back? Would she have been able to live an entire year on the future value of $130,000? How long did it take her to save up the $50,000 she used to pay off her debt? Is it possible that she may have to work a couple more years in retirement in order to make up for the loss of that money?

Of course, I wholeheartedly agree that paying off her credit card debt should have been her priority, but not at the expense of her future retirement. What would that have looked like? She would have had to cut back spending in other areas and create an aggressive plan to get herself out of debt instead of robbing from her future, happy, retired self in order to pay for the decision to spend outside her means. Unfortunately, it is likely that pulling money from her retirement savings was merely a short-term fix for her issue of overspending. Do you think she stopped spending? More than likely, her lifestyle hasn't changed much, because she didn't do the work required to make lasting changes.

Please make a promise to yourself right now. Repeat after me, "I will never, ever, ever, ever, ever, ever take money out of my retirement accounts for anything other than living a comfortable retirement after I retire."

If I stopped you from doing something you'll regret for years to come, I'm a happy girl, and it was worth it.

Time for a five-minute visualization exercise.

I want you to go back to your sacred meditation space.

Take three deep breaths and close your eyes.

I'd like you to visualize your new emergency fund— the account that you gave a name to. I'm visualizing my F.R.E.E.D.O.M. fund. I also want you to visualize your retirement accounts as they look in the future.

What does it look like to have saved six months of living expenses? Visualize the dollar amount you've saved (whatever your goal for those accounts was). Visualize that you physically have that amount right now. Take a look at the numbers on your statement; it just arrived in the mail.

Pay attention to how it feels to have accumulated enough wealth to live a comfortable retirement. Do you feel free? Safe? Calm? Happy? Excited? Limitless? Powerful? Alive? Expansive?

Whatever those feelings are, I want you to sit and relax in those feelings for five minutes.

Anything is possible in this space. Your life is limitless. You're a powerful creator and a magnificent attractor. You have endless reserves available to you. You are free. You are alive. You are abundant. You are healthy. You are wealthy. You are wise. You are taken care of. The universe is abundant and expansive, and you have access to all that you've ever dreamed of.

Congratulations! In this chapter, you've learned the importance of having a backup plan for emergencies. You have a full understanding of what constitutes a true emergency and you've taken the crucial step of starting your emergency fund, which is key to owning your financial future and living a life of freedom. You've also learned the one thing you are never to do to your future self. Remember to be easy with yourself as you begin.

Change is not always easy—but with the right mindset, you will be able to enjoy your new healthy financial decisions. Set the intention that you will enjoy the journey and have fun building up your account balance and watching it grow. Perhaps you can even make a game out of it. After all, don't we play fun games to pass the time when we're on a long road trip?

Chapter 11:

Out of Balance?

"Know what you own, and know why you own it."

~ **Peter Lynch**

In this chapter, I'm going to cover several types of diversification and the benefits of each. You're going to learn about different types of investment accounts and how each of them is taxed, as well as the benefits of having different multiple investment accounts as you plan for retirement. We're also going to discuss the importance of making sure the investments you hold inside of those accounts are diversified, and finally, I'm going to explain why working with one advisor whom you trust may benefit you, especially if you're one of those people who think you're diversified simply by having multiple advisors.

Investopedia defines diversification as "a risk management strategy that mixes a wide variety of investments within a portfolio. The rationale behind this technique is that a portfolio constructed of different kinds of assets will, on average, yield higher long-term returns and lower the risk of any individual holding or security."

Diversification. What comes to your mind when you hear the word? Perhaps you may have heard your parents or grandparents say things like, "Don't put all your eggs into one basket." They were most likely trying to illustrate using an example of a farmer or farmer's wife like I was. Picture Zsa Zsa Gabor with a basket full of eggs in hand. If Zsa Zsa gathered all of the eggs from the chicken shed and put them into one basket, and the basket was knocked out of her hands, she would have had a basket of broken eggs and a big mess to clean up in the chicken coup. Gross.

I prefer to explain diversification using the word bucket instead of basket (same premise).

First of all, I need to define what I mean when I say "bucket."

For our purposes, we are going to discuss the different types of "buckets" you are likely to own in your portfolio—whether now or in the future.

Many of us have money in a 401K, 403b, or other employer retirement plan. I want you to think of this account as a "bucket of money."

You may also have a Traditional IRA—that would be another bucket of money.

If you have a ROTH IRA, you own another bucket.

If you have money in a taxable (non-retirement) brokerage account, that is yet another bucket of money.

Now, I want you to take a minute and think about the types of accounts you own.

Exercise

Take a piece of paper and draw a bucket for each of your accounts and label them.

- 401K, 403b, or other retirement plan
- IRA
- ROTH
- Taxable investment account
- Savings account
- Checking account

How many buckets do you own?

Now, it's important for you to understand that each of these buckets hold money, and most of the time, that money is invested into products like mutual funds, stocks, ETFs (exchange traded funds) bonds, money market funds, and annuities.

Just because you own different buckets of money, does not mean that your investments are diversified. Let me explain.

Each of these buckets is taxed differently.

- A 401K or 403b plan and a traditional IRA are considered tax-deferred. This means that you have never paid taxes on the money sitting in those buckets. The taxes are deferred until later (hopefully during retirement when you are in a lesser tax bracket). All money withdrawn from these accounts will trigger a tax consequence. And later, when you reach age seventy-and-a-half, Uncle Sam will require you to begin taking annual withdrawals called "required minimum withdrawals"—he wants his taxes paid at some point.

- ROTH IRA contributions are considered after-tax contributions. Meaning, you've already paid the taxes before contributing to this bucket. The beauty of owning investments in this type of bucket is that you likely won't pay tax on the growth of these investments when you withdraw the money.

- Taxable or brokerage accounts are non-retirement accounts. Again, you've already paid the taxes on the money before putting it into this bucket, but you will be responsible for paying taxes on the investments as they grow, and when these investments produce dividends, interest, and/or capital gains, they are reported annually on your 1099. Think of this bucket as a "pay as you go bucket."

The more of these buckets you own, the better. Why? Because the more buckets you own, the more choices you have. During retirement, when you need money, you will be able to choose which type of bucket you want to withdraw your money from, depending on your tax situation.

For instance, twenty years down the road, if you decide to take $50,000 out of one of your buckets in order to pay for a new vehicle, if you pull it out of an IRA, you will pay federal and state tax at your current tax rate. Let's say that you will pay 15% federal and 5% state tax. You'll most likely want to have 20% withheld back for taxes before you write a check for your new car. (That's $10,000 that would be withheld before you withdraw your money.)

If you decide to pull that same $50,000 out of your ROTH bucket, you most likely won't be required to pay taxes, and you could write a check to the car dealership for $50,000.

Don't get me wrong, I am in no way, shape, or form saying that 401K plans or IRAs are a bad thing. In fact, I recommended you to try your best to max out your retirement contributions. When you contribute to your 401K plan, you have the opportunity to contribute a larger sum of money, since you're deferring the taxes until later on in hopes you'll be in a lesser tax bracket during retirement.

However, if you have the opportunity to contribute to a ROTH 401K through your employer, and you've been filling your 401K pre-tax bucket up for many years, you may want to consider contributing to a new ROTH bucket—for the purpose of what I will call tax diversification. However, this is for educational purposes only, and I cannot provide you with any tax advice—you will want to consult with your tax professional before you make any decisions.

As we discussed earlier, in addition to contributing to your employer plan each year, if you or your spouse have earned income, you are eligible to contribute to an IRA, and depending on gross adjusted income, you may be eligible to contribute to a ROTH IRA.

Contribution Limits in 2019

Here are the annual IRA contribution limits for 2019:

- Age forty-nine and under: $6,000
- Age fifty and over: $7,000 (which includes a $1,000 catch-up contribution)

Now that you have an understanding that your buckets are simply a container used to hold your investments, let's take a look at the word "diversification" again.

What investments do you hold inside of each of your buckets? Cash? Mutual funds? ETFs? Individual equities/stocks? CDs?

Do you have mutual funds in each bucket? Are the mutual funds the same, or are they different? Do you know?

This is where it gets a bit tricky, because most people know whether they have a 401K plan and an IRA, but if asked what investments they hold inside of these buckets, most don't have any idea.

What is important here:

- The investments in your 401K, IRA, ROTH, and taxable buckets need to align with your objectives. Remember we discussed objectives earlier. Were you conservative, balanced, or aggressive? Or somewhere in between?

- After you've identified your goal, desired risk, and timeline, you will be able to set a clear objective and have the opportunity to choose from multiple investment types. This is where we don't want too many eggs in one basket. This is where true diversification is key.

  » For example: You would not want to put all of your retirement money into your company stock. I have seen this way too many times. What happens if your company goes belly up? Your entire retirement savings go down with it. Your eggs are all broken along with your basket.

To illustrate this point, let's take a look at the well-known Enron scandal. If you were an employee of Enron back in 2001 and had your entire retirement savings invested into the company stock program, you may have owned shares that were trading at a high of $90.75. However, the collapse of the company on December 2, 2001 left shares trading at $0.26. Can you imagine those employees having all of their retirement money completely tied up into shares of Enron when that happened?

We all should have learned a lesson from this example when it rocked the airwaves and ended up being broadcast on every television network in the country. However, many people still have way too much of their retirement assets wrapped up into their employee stock programs. Too many eggs in one basket.

Let's regroup. At this point, if you are feeling lost, I'd like to encourage you to find a financial advisor to help you with the investment piece of your plan. You've done most of the heavy lifting already, and you should feel very proud of yourself. Find someone you feel comfortable with and whom you can trust. A good financial advisor will take all of the information you've pulled together in your fabulous new binder and plug those numbers into a formal retirement analysis program for you. He or she should be excited to take you by the hand and customize a plan to align with your goals. And if you prefer working with a female, we are growing in number. We are still outnumbered approximately eighty percent men to twenty women, but the industry is changing; I think this is a sign that women are rising up to take control of their finances and helping other women do the same.

Before we move on, I'd like to bust through a flawed premise surrounding the subject of diversification. Having accounts with multiple different financial advisors, banks, or firms does not mean that you are diversified. In fact, it may even be harmful to your overall portfolio. Why? When you have multiple advisors, each one managing only a slice of your overall pie - what happens if each of them invested their respective slice of your pie the same way? You would have no diversification. What if each slice of the pie was too aggressive? Or they were all too conservative? One hand may have no idea what the other is doing. How in the world could they do what is best for you when they don't have a view of your entire financial picture?

You may want to consider consolidating your investment accounts with one financial advisor; someone who listens to you, someone you can trust, and someone who takes the time to explain things in a way that you can understand. Allow that person to take a look at your entire financial picture, and then work with you to put together a beautiful plan designed to help you achieve your goals.

Can you imagine the peace of mind that will come from having that kind of plan in place?

In this chapter, you learned the different types of diversification. Here is what I'd like you to remember:

1. Owning different buckets for tax diversification is a beautiful thing (401K, 403b, IRA, ROTH, taxable). It will provide you with more choices in retirement.

2. Inside your buckets live your investments. Make sure these are diversified according to your objective and tolerance for risk.

3. Consolidating all of your buckets with someone you can trust will allow them to see your entire picture and help ensure you are truly diversified.

Let's do a check-in to see how you're feeling. Do you feel good? Or are you feeling a little out of balance?

I want you to write down three things you've learned from this discussion.

Now, write down one thing you intend to do in order to ensure your assets/accounts are diversified and in balance.

And finally, I want you to write down one thing you can do right now to bring balance and wellbeing to your mind, body, and soul. If you need a little help, go back to our chapter on abundance and self-care.

Great job. You're doing amazing work. You've got this!

Chapter 12:

Is Timing Everything?

"The closer you are to alignment with what you want the calmer it feels."
~Esther Hicks

No matter which side of the political fence you find yourself on, we can all agree on one thing. Every single day when we turn on our television, we are bombarded with drama and negativity. Of course, drama sells and networks chase ratings. We can all get sucked in to the drama. Remember how we were all glued to our TV sets during the OJ Simpson car chase, the terrorist attacks on 9/11, even the Weather Channel when there is a hurricane on the other side of the country (which by the way, there is right now. Hurricane Dorian is wreaking havoc as we speak and I've got the Weather Channel on in the background)? We are drawn to big experiences. They get our attention. Some are positive and some are negative. We don't find our media reporting on many positive stories. When we come across a positive story on social media, we love to post and share those feel-good stories. Conversely, we also post the crazy dramatic stories that come across our FB feed.

The stock market fluctuates up and down daily. And you may have noticed more volatility or *movement* over the past year or so, which has a lot to do with what is reported on the news every day. Trade wars, tariffs, tweets, North Korea—all of these stories play a part in what I'm going to refer to as "market noise."

I'm going to ask you to begin to tune out the noise you hear every day as you're watching CNN, NBC, CBS, FOX, Bloomberg, all of it. Why? because, at the end of the day, you are not worried about what is happening today. In fact, you should not be worried at all. If you have a solid investment plan in place, there should be little concern over what is happening on a daily, monthly, or even annual basis. When you have a solid plan, you should be confident in it and learn to tune out the noise and ride the waves.

There are a few key things to remember, and if you focus on these fundamentals, you will come out ahead of those who are sitting in their office making snap decisions based on what they see on the news (that is sometimes referred to as "timing the market" or "day trading," and this is not something you want to be doing).

Think about this with me for a moment.

When you go to the grocery store, do you like to buy things on sale, or do you like to pay the highest price? Of course, we know the answer—you want to buy on sale.

Using this concept, why would you want to jump into the market when it's at an all-time high?

And why on earth would you want to sell or get out of the market when it's down?

If you were selling your home, would you want to sell it for more than you paid for it and hopefully receive the equity you've invested into your home? Or do you want to sell it for less than you paid for it?

It is the same thing. But for some reason, investors are much too emotional about the market, and they allow themselves to be swayed by the noise. When investors get emotional, they often try to time the market. This can be one of the most detrimental, self-sabotaging things you can do.

> *"Be scared when people are greedy, and be greedy when people are scared."*
> **– Warren Buffet**

In January 2017, the Dow Jones Industrial Average hit 20,000 for the first time in history. In fact, I thought that was such a momentous event that I framed the front page of the Wall Street Journal and have it hanging on my wall.

As I am sitting here writing this book, the date is June 16, 2019. It's a Sunday, today, so the markets are closed, but on Friday afternoon at closing, the Dow was at 26,089.

A friend of mine—we'll call her Chloe—pulled all of her money out of her investments back in 2017 because she was worried that the market was at an all-time high. She kept her money in cash, and it has been sitting there for two years while she waits for the market to "crash." When Chloe took her money out of her 401k investments, she missed the growth of a 6,000-point climb on the DOW. And worse yet, her cash is most likely not even earning her 1% while it sits there.

Those who are worried about a market correction should keep in mind that over the last thirty years, the Standard and Poor's 500-stock index has only been negative in five out of thirty years. That means the market has been positive 83% of the time.

It is difficult not to be emotional about your money. In fact, there are entire books written about the phenomenon of emotional investing. And to that point, one of the biggest values of working with a financial advisor is the handholding they provide during a down market.

The S&P 500 has gained more than 17% annually over the last six-and-a-half years, so it is not surprising that folks are getting a little nervous. After all, how long can this bull market go on before we have a crash or a recession? Right?

I'm going to repeat myself—please try to drown out the noise and stay the course. There will be up years and down years. Historically, there are many more up years than there are down years. Is it fun to open your statements when your balance takes a dip? No. But, I want you to ask yourself a question—are you still contributing to your 401K or IRA plan? If the answer is yes, and it should be, then guess what, you've just gone to the grocery store during a big sale. You're buying low. You're getting more for your money. This is a good thing. Would you rather have the market be high during your entire contributing years and pay premium dollar for everything? Not me. I want more bang for my buck while I'm contributing to my 401K. And when the market goes back up, so will my account balance.

Are you a long-term investor? Your answer should be yes if you're planning for retirement. If you're a long-term investor, then you owe it to yourself to take the emotion out of the equation. Long-term investors look for the *average* return. They don't focus on their annual return—that can bounce around from year to year; what we care about is the average annual return.

The Secret to Investing: The Rule of 72

Have you heard of the Rule of 72? In my opinion, this is one of the greatest secrets of investing. Investopedia states, "The rule applies to the exponential growth of an investment based on the compounded rate of return."

There is some simple math involved here—don't panic, it's basic division.

If you take 72 and divide it by your average annual rate of return, it will provide you with the number of years it will take to double your money.

For example, if an investment yields an 7% average annual compounded rate of return, it will take approximately (72 divided by 7) 10 years to double the invested money.

Now, consider this astounding fact:

If you use my earlier example where Chloe pulled all of her money out of the market and placed it safely into a money market account paying less than 1%—let's do the math.

(72 divided by 1) = 72 years to double her invested money.

By the way, her account had been earning an average of 7% before she made the decision to sell her investments and pull out of the market. If she hadn't done that, here is what may have happened with her investments.

(72 divided by 7) equals 10 years to double her invested money.

This is one of the biggest mistakes emotional investors can make.

I'd like for you to repeat after me—"I will never try to time the market. I will not panic during a down-turn in the market. In fact, I will get excited and commit to investing more when that happens, because I will be buying low."

By now, I hope I've convinced you to get in and stay the course, no matter what the market is doing; however, if you need a little more convincing, I'd like to share with you some results from the Dalbar Study. Feel free to google it. Here are a few key findings:

- The average equity mutual fund investor underperformed the S&P 500 Index by a margin of 4.7%. While the broader market made gains of 11.96%, the average equity investor's return was only 7.26%.

- The average fixed-income mutual fund investor underperformed the Bloomberg Barclays Aggregate Bond Index by a margin of 1.42%. The broader bond market realized a return of 2.65%, while the average fixed-income fund investor's return was 1.23%.

- The twenty-year annualized S&P 500 return was 7.68%, and the average equity fund investor's was only 4.79%, a gap of 2.89%.

Why did the average investor underperform? Because he/she allowed emotions to get the best of them and tried to time the market—going in and out when they thought it was the best. Instead of just getting in and staying the course and continuing to invest systematically along the way.

In this chapter, you learned the biggest mistakes made by emotional investors. I hope I've shed some light on market volatility, and I've given you some staggering statistics to back it up.

Key Takeaways:

- Never try to time the market.
- Keep the emotion out of your investment decisions.
- Stay true to your plan, and don't allow yourself to get caught up in *market noise*.
- Remember the Rule of 72.
- During your investing years, get excited when the market goes down, it's a good time to buy!

Have I made my point? I'll end here with a little something I like to tell my clients.

"When you feel like throwing a brick through my window, tape a check to it."

Chapter 13:

Planning in Your Now

*"Life is available only in the present moment.
If you abandon the present moment you cannot live the
moments of your daily life deeply."*

~ Thich Nhat Hanh

Well, here you are. You've made it to the quintessential "take action" chapter. Congratulations! Would it surprise you if I told you that you've already arrived? That all of the "work" has already been accomplished?

Let's do a quick recap.

- You've worked to identify your tolerance for risk and have an investment objective in place.

- You've taken inventory of your assets—401k plans, IRAs, ROTH IRAs, taxable/non-retirement accounts, bank CDs, savings and cash accounts. And you've identified your average annual return on investment for each.

- You've gotten real with your spending and have a good idea what you're spending annually and where you may

123

be able to eliminate some non-essentials in order to reallocate that money toward debt reduction, savings, and investments.

- You've taken an inventory of your debt and created a plan to eliminate credit card debt as soon as possible, working to eliminate cards with the highest interest rate first. If you need more help with this one, there are many resources online. Google debt reduction snowball method.

- You know how much money you earn, and you've made the decision that you will begin to pay yourself before you pay any other company or human being on the planet.

- You've opened, named, and funded a new "emergency fund" or F.R.E.E.D.O.M. fund account.

- You have identified a target retirement date goal.

- And finally, you've combined all of the information gathered, placed it in a fabulous three-ring binder for safekeeping, and then plugged it into a retirement calculator. And you now know exactly how much money you'll need to have saved in order to live the retirement you're dreaming of.

With this information assembled, you have everything you need in order to create a personalized, solid, strategic investment plan. Do you have any idea what you've just accomplished here? You have just intimately acquainted yourself with your finances. Doesn't it feel good? Never again will you feel lost and out of control of your finances. Never again will you allow yourself to cower in fear and bury your head in the sand because you feel inadequate or because it is so overwhelming that you don't know where to start. You've done it. You've done the work. You've taken the steps necessary to be a good steward of all that you've been blessed with. And no matter if you're on track to achieve your goal on time or not, you know where you stand in your now. And there is true power in that knowledge.

You've got a plan in place, and if you don't, you're going to seek out an advisor who can help you wrap it all together and put a bow on it. Perfect. Easy button. Done.

Well, almost. You've done such a beautiful job getting to this point. Now it's time for you to learn the principles of compounding, and I think you're going to get even more excited about what you're doing. Now that you understand the basic principles of investing and have a plan in place, we're going to discuss how you can teach what you've learned to your children and your grandchildren and have an impact on generations to come. Can you visualize the wonderful feeling of teaching your children the secrets to achieving financial freedom of their own? I've done this with my children, and it has been one of the most wonderful experiences I've had in my role as a mother. We're also going to discuss compounding as it relates to the Law of Creation process. This is going to be fun.

Compounding: Money Miracles

I am going to share with you what I would call a miracle, but it's just the phenomenon of something we call compounding.

Do any of you have grandchildren who were born this year? If so, you'll be excited about what I'm going to share with you.

In this example, grandparents or parents open an account for baby who is one year old. Collectively, they contribute $1,000 to get it started. Take a look at this magic.

- $1,000 contribution into a growth mutual fund at one year old
- Let's say baby's account earns an average of 7%
- They never contribute another dollar to her account
- The account is left alone until baby (now adult) retires at sixty-five
- The account grows to $75,955 by age sixty-five
- Let's take the same scenario only let's contribute $50/month over the same sixty-five years
- $1,000 contribution at birth
- $50 per month is added for sixty-five years
- The account grows to a staggering: $718,435
- Is this a miracle? No, it's the law of compounding.
- Why weren't we taught this when our children were born? Now we know and now we need to teach this to our children and our grandchildren.
- Let's take that same $1,000, and let's begin when the child turns twenty-one and starts working.
- $1,000 contribution into a growth mutual fund at twenty-one years old
- Let's say her account earns an average of 7%
- She never contributes another dollar to the account.
- Account is left alone until age sixty-five
- Account grows to $19,628

If that same twenty-one-year old contributes $50 per month to his/her account until age sixty-five the result?

$179,300

The difference in outcome is staggering, isn't it?

The moral of the story is that it is your job to teach your children and your grandchildren these principles as early as possible.

- Begin investing as early as possible
- Make regular monthly, systematic contributions

You can play around with the numbers using a retirement calculator online. It's really fun!

As I told you way back at the beginning of our journey, I have five children. Four of them are now out in the working world, and I have taught them these principles. Each have opened ROTH IRAs and are contributing $200 per month to their plans. Unfortunately, I didn't know what I know today when they were born. We got them started in their twenties, which is earlier than most of us started.

They are contributing to their 401K plans at work, and in addition, they are working on their ROTH buckets. I could not be prouder of them.

Let's take one more example that I just used with my nineteen-year-old son, Nicholas, who is doing a summer internship as an electrician right now.

- Nick has $10,000 saved from helping farm with his father
- He plans to contribute at least $100 per month until he turns age sixty-five

- He invested into a growth portfolio and hopes to earn an average of 7%
- If he leaves it alone, and never touches a dime he should have approximately $592,828 when he turns sixty-five.

And folks, this is how it's done. We have destroyed the premise that you have to be born into money. We have destroyed the notion that you have to work hard and earn millions of dollars a year in order to be wealthy. It's all about time in the market and consistency.

By now, you may have the urge to go back and *tweak* your plan based on the fact that you still have another ten to fifteen years to take advantage of the compounding phenomenon before you retire, and that's fantastic. Do that.

With that being said, the next action we're going to discuss in our "take action" chapter, is not going to have anything to do with any of the hard work and efforting you've done in order to get here. In fact, I'm going to ask you to do the complete opposite. I'm going to ask you to let all of that stuff go. Just breathe.

I'm going to ask you to open your mind and think of compounding in a completely different way.

Let's have a chat about your thoughts and feelings again.

Thoughts turn into things. How? Let's call it the Law of Compounding.

Think back to that one-year old baby with $1,000. If her parents would have put that same $1,000 into a savings account earning less than 1% interest and kept it there for sixty-five years, it would not have been worth much more $1,000 (at 1% interest, it would have been worth $1,890).

However, when it was compounding with an average of 7% interest, it gained momentum. Lots of momentum.

The same thing happens with our thoughts.

We have thousands of thoughts every day. Many of them don't get too much of our attention and we don't assign much emotion to most of the thoughts we think. But aren't there certain subjects that receive much more of our time and attention? Most likely in the areas of money, family, relationships, career, and health, right? It's easy to identify what we're spending our time and attention on. In fact, as I'm writing this chapter, I have unwanted thoughts about a conversation I had with someone today. I just can't seem to shake the thoughts. It's as if my thoughts have taken on a life of their own. Ugh.

But why? And how did that happen? Well, I allowed it to happen because I was careless with my initial reaction to the conversation. I didn't pay attention to my internal GPS (my emotional guidance system).

When we feel good feelings about a subject, we are in alignment with our inner being. How can we tell? Because we feel happy, expansive, free, joyful, positive, energetic, creative, and loving.

When we feel bad feelings about a subject, we are out of alignment with our inner being. It is like our GPS is saying, "Warning, Will Robinson, you're moving into unwanted territory." And those feelings are pretty yucky. We can feel lonely, isolated, hopeless, angry, controlling, fear-full, sad, and closed off.

Over the years, I've learned that if I can identify those bad feeling thoughts as soon as they begin to rear their ugly head and shift my thinking to focus on better feeling thoughts, then I can stop that train before it picks up too much momentum.

Haven't you noticed that when you allow yourself to dwell on negative thoughts, they grow and compound—they add one negative thought unto another and then another? That, my friend, is how we know when we are negatively creating. Not only in our now reality, but we are creating thoughts to things for our future as well.

Don't believe me? Think about it. The better it gets, the better it gets. And the worse it gets, the worse it gets. When you have a bad day and you dwell on it, doesn't it usually get even worse? You say things like, "Can anything go right today?" "If it's not one thing it's another." "I got up on the wrong side of the bed." It compounds. And you're negatively attracting more of it into your experience, the longer you stay there and the more you talk about it.

How can you learn to harness this creative energy and begin creating the things you want instead of the things you don't want? By using the practices you learned earlier to help you get into alignment and live in a state of alignment more often. The practice of daily meditation, visualization, and affirmations are a beautiful way to get back into a state of well-being—and to line up with Source.

You can learn to use your emotional GPS to quickly identify when you're negatively creating and compounding your thoughts into things that you don't want.

I believe the key to this is to be easy with it, and not to beat yourself up when those unwanted thoughts show up. In the Law of Attraction, Abraham describes it as contrast. When contrast shows up, it is like an alert system letting you know what you don't want, and when you know what you don't want, you also know what you do want (it's the opposite side of the stick). And in that moment, a rocket of desire shoots up into your Vortex of creation.

Contrast is a good thing, as long as you recognize it for what it is and move along quickly so that you are not allowing your thoughts to begin that compounding process.

Thoughts turn into things. Anything you've imagined is already created in a vibrational escrow for you, whether positive or negative. When you focus with emotion (in a feeling state), you have the power to manifest your thoughts into your physical reality.

Momentum happens when you compound those thoughts (powered by emotion), one on top on another and then another until you believe your thoughts so strongly, they then have the power to take shape into physical form. Again, this can be positive momentum or negative momentum, so be sure that you're not negatively creating in your experience. Catching hold of negative thoughts early on and identifying what feels good and what doesn't feel good, by using your built-in emotional GPS to identify when you're off-course, is the way to stop the momentum from happening—therefore you stop creating unwanted things in your experience.

What if you allowed yourself to be more intentional with your thoughts? What could happen if you learned to harness your thoughts in a way that placed pure, positive emotion behind them and then added the belief that you can be, do, or have anything you can think or imagine?

I believe that you can. I believe that if you can think it, you can create it. Because if you have thought about it, it is already created and waiting for you in your Vortex of creation. Your storehouse. Waiting in vibrational escrow for you to combine thoughts, emotion, and belief behind it—and then allowing it to show up in your experience.

We are powerful and creative beings, and we've been blessed with beautiful thinking mechanisms called a brain. I think we've been conditioned to be lazy in our thinking, we've been conditioned to complain and wear our exhaustion and indifference like a badge of honor. Aren't you tired of living like that? Don't you want to be more intentional with the life you've been given? I do.

Should we start a movement? What would happen if we stopped complaining? What would happen if we started speaking life into what we do want instead of what we don't want? What would happen if we taught this to our children and grandchildren?

I wonder what the compounding effect would look like as it rippled out into the world around us.

And since this book is about you living the retirement of your dreams, what would happen if you allowed yourself to consistently deposit positive thoughts and feelings into your vibrational account? What would happen if you made the decision to sit down and visualize your dreams and think so many beautiful thoughts about them that they began to compound one to another until the momentum was so strong that it produced such intense feelings inside of you, until you had no choice but to believe your dream into reality? Bam. There's the magic.

In this chapter, you've learned the magic of compounding as it relates to investing as well as your thoughts and emotions—and it is my hope you've made the commitment to share it with your family, children, and grandchildren. You've completed the difficult task of creating your retirement plan, and you're doing the vibrational work to go along with your plan. I can only believe that the Universe will begin to bring the right people, places, and things into your experience and, as a result, bring your visions and dreams into reality.

I'm excited that you've learned and embraced the magic work of compounding.

Chapter 14:

Freedom or Fear?

"There is only one thing that makes a dream impossible to achieve: the fear of failure."

~ Paulo Coelho

At this point in your journey, you've traveled through all of the steps necessary in order for you to achieve financial freedom. And we've spent a lot of time talking about how to feel good while you're on your trek toward reaching that freedom. However, soon you'll put this book down and go back to your life. Before you do, let's regroup. Let's face it, there is a reason you picked up this book. Most likely, it is because you have been putting off the extremely urgent task of making sure you have a solid plan for retirement in place. Right?

Now what? Will you get around to implementing your plan? If so, when? This month? Next month? Next year? In this chapter, I'm going to share a few more true stories with you in the hopes that you will understand how critical it is that you honor yourself and follow through on the commitment you're making to show up and take ownership of your financial health and wellbeing.

Unfortunately, I've seen way too many men and women wait to create their plan in the final hour. And when I say final hour, I mean final hour.

Allison, age sixty-five, made the decision to retire last month and realized that she didn't have a plan for an income stream during retirement. She filed for social security and will be receiving a monthly benefit of $1,500 per month.

She has a total of $300,000 in an IRA. She spends $80,000 per year.

Could she afford to stop working? Unfortunately, there is no amount of compounding that is going to get her the amount of money needed to live on with as much as she spends.

To put this into perspective, when building an income strategy in retirement, it's best practice not to withdraw more than 4% of your portfolio each year. If you've saved enough, assuming a 4% withdrawal rate, your portfolio should allow you to live comfortably, while allowing your investments to grow throughout retirement without running out of money. And if planned and executed well, the intent is that you will have money to leave to your children and grandchildren or charities of your choosing.

Let's walk through Allison's dilemma.

Allison has $300,000 saved up for retirement. If she withdraws 4% of her account annually, that is $12,000. Divide $12,000 by twelve months and this leaves her with $1,000 per month in investment income along with her Social Security check of $1,500 per month.

Allison is used to spending $80,000 per year ($6,666 per month). Where is the gap of $4,166 per month going to come from?

Allison's story is heartbreaking and is the result of little to no planning. And although her character is fictitious, her story is quite common. Why didn't Allison have a plan? Fear. Allison had no knowledge or understanding of investing. She put her head down, went to work, and buried her head in the sand until one day at the magical age of sixty-five, she made the decision to retire. She thought $300,000 was enough to retire on.

Too little. Too late.

I'll share one more story with you in the hopes that you'll remember our fictional friends and never make the same mistakes.

Tanya inherited $1M from her father when he passed away five years ago. She is in her mid-fifties. After receiving her inheritance, she began withdrawing large sums of money— house projects or money to help bail the kids out for one thing or another, and before she knew it, she had approximately $100K left in her account.

Let me show you what could have happened if she chose to keep her father's money invested and simply live off of the income produced by her investments.

Tanya had $1 million dollars invested in a balanced toward growth portfolio (60/40 objective), with an average annual return of 7%. If she had stayed invested for ten years (which would have gotten her to age sixty-five), her account may have potentially grown to $1,967,151. Had she then made the decision to begin drawing income from her portfolio, (say

4% each year), she would have had close to $80,000 a year in income for the rest of her life. Her unhealthy spending habits had catastrophic results and cost her the opportunity of financial freedom. As a result, Tanya now has to rely solely on her Social Security benefit and may even need government assistance at some point in her future. Devastating.

Wow, that was depressing. We need some good news now.

Remember our friend Madeline? We talked about her way back in the beginning of the book. The fabulous, type A personality, successful at everything she does.

She just turned fifty, and like most of us she started thinking about retirement and wondering if she was going to be prepared.

Madeline created a plan that kicked her retirement accounts into overdrive, and she's one hundred percent on track for living her dream of lying by the pool and joining her friends for golf at the club.

How did she do it?

- She decided to downsize her life a little bit. She sold her extremely expensive home in the Berkshires and eliminated the situation of being "house poor." She purchased a great little condo with much less maintenance and stress.

- She made it her mission to pay off all of her credit card debt, and she maintains a zero balance on all cards to this day. If she uses them, she pays them in full every month.

- She is contributing the max of $19K to her 401K plan, plus the annual catch up contribution of $6K, allowed for age fifty years and up.

- She is contributing $6K to her IRA and the additional $1K in catch up contribution allowed for age fifty years and up.
- She consolidated all of her old employer 401K plans into an IRA account with a total of $400K.
- She has about ten more years before she retires and isn't afraid of market fluctuations, so she invested in a growth portfolio consisting of 80% stocks/20% bonds.
- She is hoping to earn an average long-term growth of at least 9% (but she's being cautious and planning for a 7% average annual return).

Here is what her (hypothetical) portfolio could look like ten years from now.

- $400K portfolio
- Contributing $32K/year for ten years
- 9% average return = $1.4M
- 7% average return = $1.2M
- She's eliminated debt. She lives within her means.

If she decides she wants to work until age sixty-five, here is what it could look like.

- $400K portfolio
- Contributing $32K/year for fifteen years
- 9% average return = $2.4M
- 7% average return = $1.9M

My guess is that she will continue to work some consulting gig and enjoy being semi-retired from age sixty to sixty-five. But you know what? She has given herself the gift of choice. And that's true F.R.E.E.D.O.M.

Better yet, she's been meditating in the morning before work and she's manifested a super cool human man into her life. She is taking good care of herself and enjoying her life. And she's working on not only compounding her money in a positive direction, but her thoughts, words, and feelings, too.

Not only will she be able to retire on her terms, but she's going to have money to leave to her sweet niece, whom she adores.

Let's review the top ten reasons people fail to reach their retirement goals:

1. Life happens, and they take money out of their retirement plan to cover debt, mostly due to out of control spending habits.
2. They don't contribute enough money to their plan during high earning years.
3. They don't start early enough.
4. They don't contribute consistently. Every paycheck. Every month. Every year.
5. They spend too much money.
6. They incur too much debt.
7. They try to invest on their own, and panic during market fluctuations and pull money out at the worst time—the market low—and jump back in when the market is high.
8. They try to invest on their own and try to time the market instead of just getting in and staying the course.

9. They keep all of their money in low earning investments like CDs.
10. They lose half of their assets in a divorce.

What have you learned in this chapter? Moral of the story: don't be afraid. No matter where you are. Get in there and make it happen. Don't wait one more day to take action. Every day, month, and year that goes by, you're giving up the time needed for the magic of compounding to work for you. You've got this. I believe in you. Your freedom depends upon it.

Chapter 15:

The Rest Is Still Unwritten

"You didn't come for the manifestation—you came for the manifesting. You didn't come for the creation—you came for the creating. You came because you are a Creator and a Creator's gotta create."

~ Abraham - Hicks

Well, we've had quite a ride together, haven't we? I told you, way back in Chapter 3, that I am all about the experience, and I have loved every minute of helping you prepare for your journey.

Thank you for graciously listening to my story; I am so happy to have been even a small part of yours. Your story is one of grace, strength, and love. My wish for you is that you will begin to be as kind and generous to yourself as you are with everyone else around you. Remember, you belong to a tribe of brilliant, talented, beautiful women who, like you, have made the decision to take ownership of their financial future. Women who intend to be more intentional in how we show up in the world. Women who will no longer hide in the shadows and let others make financial decisions for them. No, our tribe of women will not only handle our business, but we will teach our children to do the same. Our tribe is a tribe of powerful creators, attractors, and allowers—and the Universe is partnering with us every bit of the way.

It's time to pop the champagne and toast to your success!

As I watch you go, I am imagining your Vortex of creation releasing beautiful surprises and delights into your experience all along your path—your GPS is in place, and you've learned everything you need to know in order to get to your dream destination.

Congratulations! You've taken ownership of your financial future. You've spent the last seven chapters learning and implementing the "F.R.E.E.D.O.M" process. Let's review what you've learned and how far you've come.

F: You've learned the value of putting yourself first. You're learned it's okay to be selfish.

You've decided that selfish is not a dirty word. You got real about your relationship with your money and made the decision to begin—and you took the first steps in planning, organizing, and gaining control of your finances. You gained clarity around your commitment to creating a plan and made the decision to stick to it.

R: You understand the concepts of risk and reward—in a way that makes sense to you.

You learned the importance of having clearly articulated goals as well as setting the timeframe for achieving your goals. You understand the importance of aligning your goals with your tolerance for risk, and finally, took a look at types of investment options and the differences between them. You now have a better understanding of the concept of risk and how it plays a part in your overall strategy.

E: You know where you want to go and you're starting with the end in mind.

In this chapter, you allowed yourself the sacred space and time to dream a little. I walked you through a visualization exercise that allowed you to get lost in dreaming about your deepest desires. You gained some inspiration into what you want your dream retirement to look like, and I walked you through a list of actionable steps that led you to an understanding of where you currently stand financially and where you would like to be at retirement age.

E: You've made the wise decision to plan for emergencies—because life happens.

In this chapter, we not only discussed the importance of having a backup plan in place for when life happens—we created your emergency fund. Not only do you understand why you need one—you know how to use it, you're committed to building it up, and you understand that it can only be used in the case of a true emergency. Wow. That feels like freedom to me!

D: You understand the value of diversification and the beauty of balance.

Here we sorted out the different types of diversification and the benefits of each. You learned about different type of investment accounts and how each of them is taxed, as well as the benefits of having multiple buckets as you plan for retirement. We discussed the importance of diversification of the investments you hold inside of those buckets, and finally, I explained why working with a single advisor may be of benefit you.

O: Oh no. You're never going to panic when the market gets noisy.

In this next chapter, I revealed to you one of the most detrimental and self-sabotaging mistakes investors can make. I've shed some light on market volatility (which I refer to as noise), and you are now armed with the knowledge necessary to make informed decisions about your money and will never allow yourself to get swept away by your emotions. You've learned all about the Rule of 72. And you strengthened your resolve to stay the course without deviating from your plan.

M: You've made the decision to move it and you're headed in the direction of your dreams.

In our final step, you learned the principles and magic of compounding (financially, as well as how it relates to your thoughts and emotions), and you've made the decision not only to take full and complete ownership of your financial health and wellbeing, you've committed to sharing your new knowledge with your children and your grandchildren, which will have a ripple effect for generations to come.

I'm so excited that you've made the decision to take ownership of your financial future. My hope is that, along the way, you've recognized how powerful and beautiful you are. My desire is that you've begun to incorporate daily rituals and powerful practices that lift your soul and raise your vibration as you show up in a new way, full of energy and fresh excitement every morning. You've taken your power back, Sister. I hope I've inspired you to selfishly and without guilt create space for yourself with a knowing and deep understanding that the Universe is abundant, and as Author Gabrielle Bernstein says in her book, *The Universe Has Your Back.*

What are you waiting for? It's time for you to get in the car and drive the rest of the way. You've decided where you want to go for your dream destination, and you've mapped out how to get there. It's time for you to navigate the rest of the way. Please remember to put enough gas in your tank so that you don't run on fumes, or even worse, run empty. I want you to make it there safely and on time.

Please watch your speed. If you drive too fast, you may end up with a ticket. Don't get too aggressive with your driving, or you may wreck your beautiful car. On the other hand, don't drive *too* slow, or you may not get to your destination on time. Follow the signs and speed limit—according to your objective of arriving happy and refreshed at your destination.

Most importantly, turn the radio on, sing at the top of your lungs, and stop to enjoy the beautiful sights along the way. Notice the skyline and offer a prayer of thanksgiving and gratitude for all that you've been blessed with.

If you lose your way, or take a wrong turn, no worries. Be easy with yourself, laugh it off, turn your car around, and get back on the highway.

Yep—there I went with that road trip analogy again.

Your story is still unfolding—and the rest is still unwritten. Drop me a post card to let me know where you end up. I can't wait to hear about all of the amazing things you experience along the way.

You are a powerful woman with a plan. You are unstoppable.

Acknowledgments

When I was a little girl, I would lay flat on my back in the middle of our driveway, as the hot Florida sun was going down, giving reprieve from the heat of the day. I would gaze up at the clouds feeling the support of the cool cement underneath my body. Somehow, I innately knew that the Universe was a supportive, expansive, and magical place. I used to look up at the sky and dream dreams of exploring the world and traveling to distant lands. I was a dreamer. Looking back, I wonder if I wasn't already practicing meditation and visualization. Do we somehow unlearn these things as we begin to adult? I knew I was special. I knew I was meant for more. I knew I came here to live an extraordinary life.

I've been on an amazing journey of exploration, that's for sure, and much of it has netted out extremely difficult, yet valuable lessons. I am grateful for all of the disaster and difficulties I've experienced along the way, for they have brought me to this beautiful place that I now stand—and in the process I've gained wisdom, learned to trust Universal abundance, and have taken my power back. I now stand strong in the belief that things are always working out for me.

To The Author Incubator team: A special thank you to Dr. Angela Lauria, CEO and founder of The Author Incubator, for believing in me and my message and pushing me to show up and be the person who wrote this book—you are not only brilliant, you are a true visionary, powerful attractor, and literary genius. To my developmental editor, Mehrina Asif, and my managing Editor, Cory Hott, thanks for making the process seamless and guiding me along my book writing journey. Cory, there are few humans in this world who have the ability to look into the soul of an author, recognize their greatness, and pull it out to make it shine for the world to see. You have this ability and I am so honored to have the privilege of calling you friend, as well as being the recipient of your mad editorial ninja magic.

Thank you to David Hancock and the Morgan James Publishing team for helping me bring this book to print.

To my tribe of forever friends –

Shannon Ionata , Jene' Cox, Liz Leeseberg, Leann Berte, Holli Condoleon, Amy Wolter, Niesha Muller, Mindy Erpelding, Kim Reutzel, Carla Skow, Kim Weaver, Shannon Goche, Carol Heesch, Sandee Vaske, Kathy Zich, Annmarie Molina, Jackie Hopkins, Mollie Becker, Kathy Nokleby, Carolyn Frakes, Mary Jane Keith, Nicole Fritz-Kemna, Jane Frankl, Margi Lantos, Cathy Berke, my dear friend and fellow Author, Lisa Earle McLeod, the entire *jane iredale* tribe, and my *seesters*, Kristina and Ava—thank you for the sacred gift of friendship. I have learned so much from each of you over the years and consider you amongst the strongest and most powerful women I know.

To my professional mentors, Bob Montgomery and Theresa Robison, thank you for always pushing me to think globally and strategically. I may not have always appreciated the constant push outside of my comfort zone, but I learned so much from you over the years and believe that I am where I am today because of the knowledge gained during our years together at IMC. Theresa, you are the epitome of a powerful woman—I am honored to have worn matching superwoman bracelets and served alongside you in the trenches! And to my dearest Miss Mary O'Connor, thanks for being my partner in crime. I couldn't have done any of it without you by my side.

To my dearest guardian angel, Jane Iredale—sometimes an extraordinary person enters our life at exactly the right moment in time. For me, this is you. Thank you for gifting me an opportunity that changed the trajectory of my life and the lives of my children. I am forever grateful for the decade of experiences we had together and am completely indebted to you for the opportunity to learn, grow, and lead your organization, filled with some of the most beautiful women and humans I've ever met. Your belief in me and my abilities allowed me to progress in my career and provide for my children during some of the toughest years of my life. I pray that every bit of magic you've brought into my life flows back to you and your family for generations to come. You are one of the most powerful women I've ever known—and you've used your power for good. Thank you for modeling excellence to all of the powerful women in your organization throughout the years. You have made a difference. That's what powerful women do.

To Bill Ecskstrom, Sarah Wirth and the other ECSELL-ERS over there at the EcSell Institute, you are the epitome of excellence, leadership and professionalism. The time spent coaching with your organization netted powerful results.

To my children, Ryan and Cayla, Cori Lynn, Kyle, Nicholas and Riley—you are my everything. I love you as high as the sky, as deep as the ocean, as wide as the sea—infinity and beyond. I love you more than you love me. Thank you for putting up with me through all the years of travel and scheduled chaos. Each of you has given me the gift of unconditional love. I cannot put into words how proud I am to have been given the sacred honor of sharing space in this world with you. You are by far the most amazing humans on this planet. And Kyle Wilson—our heart journey together has honestly been the biggest catalyst to creating the powerful woman I am today. You may have been born with half of your heart, but you have the biggest, most beautiful heart I've ever known. To Andrew—we've come a long way! Thank you for being such a wonderful father to our children and friend to me. What doesn't kill us makes us stronger. You're living proof.

And to Richard—thank you for encouraging me to write this book and put my *experiences* down into words. Your love, support and belief in me has been a breath of fresh air, and our time together has not only helped me to heal from the past, you've also held my hand while I've taken on the many new and exciting challenges that will lead into the future—encouraging me every step of the way while I stand in my now. You will always have my love, respect, and appreciation. Thanks for putting up with me. I know it's not always easy. I love you and your children - Kelsie, Michael, and Anna—with all my heart.

And a very special dedication to Charles "Chuck" Berke—I have no doubt that you had a hand in this and are belting out a theatrical song of celebration from the heavens. Say hello to Grandma Bess for me. Until we meet again, my friend.

Thank You!

Thank you so much for reading *Powerful Women Plan for Retirement*. If you've made it this far, welcome to our tribe of super successful, talented creators and attractors, aka: Powerful Women.

I would love to learn more about your journey and experience of success as you begin to write your new story, create a life of abundance, and plan the retirement of your dreams.

I'd like to personally invite you to join our Powerful Women Tribe. Just visit us at https://PowerfulWomenBook.com, and click "Join the Tribe."

Cheers to your success. You are a powerful woman!

Health, Wealth + Happiness!

Debbie

To connect with me about media appearances, interviews and podcasts visit https://PowerfulWomenBook.com. Follow me on Instagram: @PowerfulWomenBook

About the Author

Debra K. Menke is a personal finance professional who specializes in helping women to take control of their financial future. Debra has helped hundreds of men, women, and young adults create personalized financial strategies and retirement plans.

During her career, Debbie noticed an alarming trend among successful professional women—most women, even those earning a six-figure income, had no idea how to plan for their retirement. She watched as they continued habits of overspending and poor planning, and made it her mission to change this trend.

Debbie decided it was time for powerful women everywhere to stand in their power and claim ownership of their future. As a result, Debbie founded the Powerful Women Coaching Academy and is committed to making a difference in the lives of women for generations to come.

Most of Debbie's career has been spent coaching female sales professionals. Before making her career shift into the financial industry, Debbie served as director of sales, U.S. and Caribbean for *jane iredale cosmetics,* the international leader among mineral cosmetic brands. During her tenure, she was tasked with the leadership and development of Jane's sales team, which over the years included hundreds of female sales professionals and managers from all over the country.

Debbie is an award-winning sales leadership coach and was recognized by the EcSell Institute as Coach of the Year in 2015.

Debbie lives in the Heartland near Des Moines, Iowa. She enjoys spending time with her five adult children and her Old English Sheepdog, Charlie.

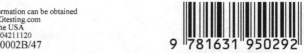